I0089985

HARD TALK

*Confessions of an Accidental Marketing
and Communications Professional*

EILEEN CASSIDY RIVERA

Foreword by JD Kathuria

Copyright © 2023 Eileen Cassidy Rivera
Published by Government Market Press

All rights reserved.
No part of this publication may be reproduced, distributed, or transmitted in any form or by any means, including photocopying, recording, or other electronic or mechanical methods, without the prior written permission of the publisher, except in the case of brief quotations embodied in critical reviews and certain other non-commercial uses permitted by copyright law.

hard talk

idiom

1. Dealing with unpleasant subjects in a truthful way, no matter how much people, or likely a group of people, may disagree.
2. A talk or discussion in which two people talk honestly and in a serious way about their feelings.

The Chronicles of Narnia, The Magician's Nephew, by C.S. Lewis

"They stared very hard at one another, trying to remember. And then, at exactly the same moment, she shouted out 'Mr. Ketterley' and he shouted out 'Uncle Andrew,' and they knew who they were and began to remember the whole story. After a few minutes of hard talking, they had got it straight."

For Kyle, Carmen, and Drew
You are my inspiration. At the end of the day,
your opinions of me matter the most.

For my late Dad
I know you're beaming down from heaven. Oh, how I
wish I could be sitting next to you right now.

For my Mom
Thank you for believing in me and being by
my side when I needed you most.

For Brian
You are the best brother. Ever.

For Andy
You are my rock and anchor in this life's ocean.

Praise for *Hard Talk*

"*Hard Talk* provides an insightful and comprehensive overview of the experiences and unique challenges Eileen faced working with and for government agencies. Eileen combines her personal and professional expertise creating a practical and informative guide based on these life experiences. *Hard Talk* is a resource for any top professional within a government agency or government partner looking to improve their public relations, communication, and marketing skills. Enhancing one's awareness and maturity in these areas is what we all should strive for by better understanding the stories and experiences of others." **David Casey, Senior Vice President, Government Relations, Maximus**

"Prior to her entry in the government contracting industry, Eileen's combination of government service, political acumen and business expertise advanced a nascent idea that corporations, foundations, educational institutions, and youth-serving organizations can successfully work together as global partners to help young people thrive and succeed. Eileen's book is a captivating story about her continuing journey to collaborate with a multitude of different interests to distill common ground toward successful outcomes**." Hon. Aaron S. Williams, Former Director, US Peace Corps**

"Eileen is a superb crisis communications professional. She's done a great job creating a practical playbook for crisis communications management through real-time experience. This compelling story illustrates the importance of integrating corporate communications across the business enterprise." **Mac Curtis, Chairman of the Board, Cubic Corporation and** former CEO of Pearson Government Solutions, Vangent, Vencore, Chairman and CEO Perspecta (NYSE: PRSP)

"Eileen's story beautifully captures an exciting time when we tackled together one of the healthcare industry's major IT challenges: the seamless integration of disparate systems to present an accurate and complete view of patient data. I am grateful to Eileen for sharing her heartfelt account and the lessons we learned. "**Vishal Agrawal, M.D., Chief Strategy and Corporate Development Officer, Humana**

"It is a major achievement to write a book that is creative, informative, and compelling reading. Eileen has managed to do just that and more, while also sharing her personal story with sensitivity and candor. Brava, my friend. We have switched roles and I now am learning from your experiences and wisdom." **Hon. Lauri Fitz-Pegado, Advocate, Advisor, and Author, Former Assistant Secretary and Director General of the US and Foreign Commercial Service**

"Eileen provides a first-rate primer on successful marketing/ communications best practices—readable, practical and full of wisdom and warmth." **Hon. Jill A Schuker, former Special Assistant to the President for National Security Affairs and Deputy Director for Communications**

"Eileen's story reinforces the reality that today, professional, and personal success is largely determined by one's willingness to embrace unexpected opportunities with courage and grit. She has beautifully captured moments of vulnerability and triumph while sharing wisdom of the MarCom trade that will benefit anyone at any level in their career." **Brandon Fureigh, Senior Director, Strategic Engagement & Communications, Oracle Health**

"GovCon communication professionals must select the best and most accurate sources on which to rely, then translate them into internal and external communications. Accurate, reliable sources are key for these professionals to provide useful information to their company, their clients and the media. Eileen Cassidy Rivera mastered these areas and is second to none in the role of a GovCon communicator. Having worked through the 9/11 crisis and now at Maximus, she exemplifies what a true communicator should be." **Mark Amtower, GovCon SME, Author, Speaker, and Podcaster**

CONTENTS

FOREWORD

On a crisp fall morning in 2007, I walked into a restaurant in Tysons Corner, Virginia. An effervescent woman was talking about marketing and communications and their evolving role in the government contracting industry. Her passion was palpable.

Little did I know this brief meeting with Eileen Cassidy Rivera would form a long-lasting friendship and professional relationship.

Over the years, our careers evolved in ways we never imagined that morning in 2007. I went on to start my own business, WashingtonExec, a thought leadership forum that helps industry and government executives build trusted relationships over the course of their careers. We started with one executive council, a meager newsletter, and a website with zero visitors. Today, we have 28 councils, 10,000+ newsletter subscribers and 80,000+ monthly website visitors.

And Eileen, then vice president of communications and investor relations at Vangent, went on to lead MarCom at some of the most well-known government contractors.

In 2012, I was considering who could lead a newly formed WashingtonExec Marketing Council. I needed someone to spark thoughtful conversations around what's referred to as "MarCom" and discuss how to develop and implement branding and communications strategies.

I asked Eileen to be chair, and she said yes.

She shared her knowledge in council meetings and in columns we published on WashingtonExec.com. Her insight was on topics like crisis communications for government contractors, the importance of creating great customer experiences, and how to take MarCom strategies to new heights.

I have been encouraging Eileen to write a book to share her two-decade journey and offer advice to those entering the government contracting, more succinctly known as the GovCon space. Our industry is at an inflection point — the confluence of emerging technologies, more emphasis on sustainability and environmental responsibility, and a changing political landscape have created a perfect storm of challenges but also opportunities.

All these factors are also leading to significant changes in the industry — and only companies that adapt and evolve will flourish in this new environment.

But what, exactly, is needed to be successful?

A key ingredient is an effective MarCom leader, as Eileen points out in this book. The future of MarCom likely involves more emphasis on digital and data-driven strategies, a laser focus on building brand awareness and credibility, as well as being able to effectively measure and analyze the return on investment, or ROI, of marketing. Transforming brands and building and maintaining reputations should be seen as crucial to increased revenue and business growth as any C-suite function.

But most importantly, the future MarCom leader will have to be someone always learning, always adapting, and always pushing the boundaries of what's possible. People who excel in it can make a real impact on the success of a company — people like Eileen.

The tools and tips in this book will help empower current and future MarCom leaders and help their GovCon companies grow, diversify, rebrand, and become market leaders. Through Eileen's narrative, she recounts both personal and professional experiences that shaped her MarCom career. Her story provides insight into a world that can only be described by those who lived it — and I think it can inspire you, too.

JD Kathuria
Founder and CEO
WashingtonExec

A STEP BACK AND A LOOK FORWARD: THE FUTURE OF MARCOM LEADERSHIP

About a decade ago, on May 31, 2013, I delivered the keynote speech at a celebration commemorating the 10th year of "Building Better Futures," a program that helps at-risk high school students in Alexandria, Virginia, prepare for college. More than 100 students participated in the program and received tutoring and advocacy services to help them plan for their future after high school. The Campagna Center, a non-profit in Alexandria, sponsored the program and has supported children and families since 1945.

The Building Better Futures program focuses on a critical section of our local community considered "at risk" — students who lack a safe and stable support network. The program assists students in visiting colleges, applying for financial aid, writing resumes, and learning interviewing skills. It also promotes community service projects. Over 80% of the students qualified for free or reduced lunch, and all participating seniors were accepted to college.

Keynoting at this important event was a huge honor. As I wrote my speech, I took an introspective look at my life and career. I traveled a long way from where I was born in Milwaukee, Wisconsin, and where I grew up in

Rochester, New York. As I prepared my remarks, I thought about my journey, the places I lived, the countries I visited, the people I met, everything I learned, and all the experiences in between.

Humbly putting everything into perspective helped me apply lessons and experiences from my journey, which I knew was very different from the students and families who would be listening to me speak that day. I wanted to share perspectives from my journey that could resonate and benefit them as they prepared for a major transition in their lives.

I vividly recall standing on stage at T.C. Williams High School (now Alexandria City High School), before a full auditorium of students, families, educators, administrators, and city leaders on a hot and humid afternoon. I helped open the school eight years prior while serving on the Alexandria City Public Schools board. I felt a special connection with the students and their families that stayed with me until this day. It was an experience I'd always remember, and I hope the students and their families did, too.

My message was about the power of courage. I recognized the parents in the audience for their sacrifices and difficult conversations to provide their children with the opportunity to achieve their dreams. I spoke of the children's potential to explore the world and accomplish great things, thanks to their parents' courage and determination.

I told stories of my high school years, when I learned foreign languages to communicate with people from other countries I hoped to visit. I saved money to travel and learn about other cultures, their challenges, and how they overcame them. My curiosity about other people's dreams and struggles led me to serve in the government, and ultimately, run for office and get elected to represent my community on the school board.

I also talked about my passion for mentoring students who aspire to pursue a career like the one I've been fortunate to forge as an award-winning corporate and government executive.

Ron Brown, the first Black chair of the Democratic Party and secretary of commerce, who I met through my mentors Lauri Fitz-Pegado and Jill Schuker, once said: "Politics, life, and business are not spectator sports. You have to get involved to get ahead. Most importantly, when you reach that level of success, keep the door open and the ladder down for others to follow."

As I wrote this book about my life and career, I aim to inspire readers to make decisions with courage and conviction, as Ron Brown did. I hope my story helps those looking for inspiration, direction, and reassurance.

I decided to start my book when I was at a crossroads, both personally and professionally. The story I share is about the 22 years following a hugely rewarding career as a political appointee in the Clinton administration serving at the Commerce Department, the Small Business Administration, and the Peace Corps, and the new career I had as a MarCom executive in the GovCon industry.

In my story, I share how I managed a new career, dealt with a painful divorce, navigated being a successful working mother in a male-dominated industry, and earned a seat at the table as a MarCom executive.

I sincerely hope my story can provide insights to those who, like me, built a career unexpectedly under unexpected circumstances. I also hope my story is useful to those who chose a career in MarCom and may relate to my experiences and can benefit from the lessons learned.

Being at the proverbial table as a MarCom leader in GovCon is a relatively new thing. Once thought of as an unnecessary overhead expense that needed to be approved in advance, communications and marketing leaders are increasingly seen as a strategic asset to companies who know it's not just about delivering services — it's about effectively communicating the value of a company's brand to a myriad of audiences, most importantly, the government client.

I hope my story will help corporate executives better understand and appreciate the confluence of skills, talents, and abilities communications and marketing leaders bring to companies — and to ensure these leaders have a presence and voice when important decisions are made.

I hope my book will help young people find a fulfilling career path in an industry that is becoming increasingly important. As the world and our nation face more complex challenges, government agencies rely more on contractors for essential services. The industry needs diverse, talented, and passionate young people to help deliver these services and share their experiences. I hope my book can be part of encouraging this important mission.

HARD TALK

CHAPTER 1

HOW THE HECK DID I GET INTO THIS LINE OF WORK, ANYWAY?

I've wanted to write a book for *a long time*. Throughout my life, I've had some unforgettable experiences, met some amazing people, and learned my share of lessons, sometimes the hard way. So many times over the years, I'd catch myself saying, *"Now, that's going in my book."*

Anyone who's written a book knows it requires finding "that time." In between working full-time, navigating my career, getting divorced, getting married, raising two kids and a stepson, getting elected and serving on the school board, having two hip replacements, being involved in my community, traveling, and doing my best to stay fit and healthy, I somehow found "that time." If it weren't for my patient husband, Andy, my family and good friends who've prodded me along the way, I'm not sure how this book would have come together.

I also wanted to prove to myself, *I could actually write and finish a book.*

And now, *I get to share my story.*

There are many places where I could have started *this story*. Perhaps, the hardest part was deciding where to begin. For *this book*, I'll start at a point that, in many ways, seemed like an ending: late January 2001.

I was going through a difficult divorce and a painful custody battle with my ex-husband. I had just left a political appointment in the Clinton administration as director of public affairs and press at the Peace Corps.

Folks who know me have long heard me say it was the best job I ever had. Going into the Peace Corps headquarters office at the corner of 20th and L streets was like being a kid in a candy store. The people were so interesting, warm, and passionate about furthering the ideals of the late President John F. Kennedy, who founded the Peace Corps at the steps of the University of Michigan on Oct. 14, 1960.

As a political appointee in the Clinton administration, I was serving at the "pleasure of the president." In my case, I was a Schedule C appointee, a type of political appointment for policy roles involving a "close and confidential working relationship" with an agency head or other top-appointed official. In other words, a Schedule C appointee can be dismissed at any time, typically when the administration ends and a new president is elected.

It was right after Election Day 2000 and the brutal 36-day legal battle over one of the most contested presidential elections in U.S. history. The landmark Supreme Court decision on Dec. 12, 2000, officially ended Vice President Al Gore's campaign against Texas Gov. George W. Bush. That's when I knew my days at the Peace Corps were numbered. The end of the Clinton administration was imminent, and I needed to find a new job.

My son, Kyle, was about to turn 3. Kyle was inquisitive, talkative, and full of sweetness. He had a knack for putting together Lego sets. I loved spending time together. When his dad and I were going through our painful split and we began to navigate an awkward custodial schedule, I made sure Kyle knew I loved him and would be there for him, no matter what.

Thanks to my close friend, Laura Lewis Mead, whom I met while we were pursuing our MBAs at American University, she recommended me for a position at Electronic Data Systems (EDS), now Hewlett Packard (HP) Enterprise as director of PR for its federal government business.

By far, it wasn't my first choice for my post-government gig.

As much as I hoped to land a role where I could leverage my passion and experience in foreign policy and international trade, I was in a new phase of my life as a single mom paying child support. Working long hours and traveling the world as I had done during the administration wasn't in the cards. Kyle was my top priority.

I took the job at EDS knowing I could be a responsible and reliable working mom. The only traveling I had to do was the challenging commute from my home in Alexandria, Virginia to EDS' offices in Herndon close to Dulles Airport. Thankfully, the compensation package allowed me to cover my new child support obligation while keeping a roof over our heads. It was a scary time, but my Catholic faith and support from my family kept me going.

As I grew my sea legs and began a new chapter of my life, my new roles widened my eyes to a new way of living and a new career in GovCon I had never imagined.

The first few months at EDS were awkward and challenging, to say the least. While I spent eight years working in the private sector before becoming a political appointee in 1993, the GovCon culture was vastly different.

For starters, I had to get a whole new wardrobe. At the Peace Corps, flowing skirts, casual tops, and comfy shoes were "the look." At EDS, women were expected to wear the "EDS uniform": suntan-colored pantyhose, navy blue suits — with skirts, not pants — white blouses and those little scarves you tie around your neck. *Really*? I thought. It wasn't a look I could pull off.

I also wasn't sure how to navigate "single shaming." Adapting to a new life as a single mom, I soon discovered the EDS culture was far more conservative than the federal government. I was getting to know my team and we inevitably talked about our personal lives and families. They asked me what my husband did, where he worked and how many kids I had. When I told them I had just gone through a divorce and had a joint custody agreement with my ex-husband, I sensed discomfort and uneasiness.

That year, I was invited to the annual holiday party and was asked to provide my husband's name for the guest list. The woman organizing the event emailed me back and said: "Eileen, that man you'd like to invite to the holiday party, he has a different last name than yours. Is he your husband?" I told her he was my boyfriend and would be my guest. She said the event was only for married couples and she'd make an exception and keep my guest and I on the list. I was shocked. Yes, that was in 2001.

Getting to know my team better eased me into what felt like landing on a new planet. My staff helped me understand the lexicon and vocabulary of GovCon. It was like another language — and far more challenging than the foreign languages I mastered during high school and college.

I was comfortable working in a matrixed environment with staff in the office and remotely in other parts of the country. But I initially struggled to wrap my head around what EDS did for the government.

I knew it was a global corporation based in Plano, Texas, founded by the late Ross Perot. A colorful personality with infamous big ears, he made a name for himself when he ran for president in 1992 and 1996. He created a successful business, building and running data processing systems known as information technology, or IT. I hadn't yet had much exposure to IT while working in the government as it was just becoming a relatively new way to connect computers, software, and systems. I jokingly told my family I barely knew how to turn a computer on when I took the job at EDS.

Bill Ritz, an affable older guy who was EDS' press director for its federal business, interviewed me for the role. I'll never forget what he said during my final interview when I shared my inexperience with computers and IT, "Eileen, I can teach you IT and government contracting, but I can't teach you PR. That's why we want to hire you."

When I first started working in this new world of IT and GovCon in 2001, less than 10% of Americans had access to the internet. Hard to believe, but most people back then used dial-up connections. Remember AOL? Websites were slowly popping up. Electronic commerce was just becoming a thing. As the world began to experience the power of the internet, the U.S. federal government needed help connecting information systems and networks, so it awarded contracts to companies like EDS to do just that.

Shortly after I joined EDS, the company won a major contract with the U.S. Navy called NMCI — the Navy/Marine Corps Intranet. At the time, it was considered the crown jewel of government contracts, in part because of the massive size of the contract and the complexity of the work it entailed. I remember reading excerpts of EDS' proposal to win the NMCI contract. Then-Secretary of the Navy Gordon England summed up the Navy's IT environment before the start of NMCI: "We basically had 28 separate commands budgeting, developing, licensing, and operating IT autonomously. It was inefficient and from the larger Department perspective, produced results that were far from optimal."

Throughout NMCI's lifespan, the program consolidated roughly 6,000 networks — some of which couldn't email, let alone collaborate, with each other — into a single, integrated, and secure IT environment. I had never heard of anything like this before.

One of my first significant projects was to work on the news release to announce EDS' huge award with the Navy. EDS' head of corporate communications in Plano asked me to prepare a "solid draft" our Navy customer would approve, that the investor community would understand, and the media would use to write good stories. I had written numerous announcements, communications, and news releases working in the federal government, but I had never crafted a press release for a government contractor.

I was familiar with messaging for multiple audiences having worked at Hill+Knowlton, the renowned global public affairs firm where I spent 4.5 after business school, as well as in the Clinton administration, but this was the first time I communicated with "the Street."

To help me understand how to prepare such communication, I looked at other "win releases" issued by EDS and press releases published by other government contractors. Win announcements weren't part of my repertoire at the Peace Corps, but they soon became a key component of my arsenal as a government contractor PR leader.

The first thing I learned about writing a win announcement was explaining the total contract value and contract term. Considered the key ingredients of a win release, getting these two pieces of information correct was paramount. With my finance and government background, I knew how to find the information, and explain and communicate the financial aspects and value of a government contract.

I also had to explain to the head of corporate communications in Plano how government contracts are paid, the budgeting cycle of federal agencies like the Defense Department, and when EDS would realize a profit. I'll never forget his incredulous reaction when I sent him the draft release and accompanying talking points. "Wait a minute, we have to wait three years to realize a profit?" he sputtered. "How will we explain that to investors?"

While it'd be a few more years (and a different company) before I formally led investor relations, or IR, I began developing a sense of how to "speak to the Street" while communicating to the trade media covering the GovCon industry. It became a skill set I'd apply to not just press releases but other strategies I later created for EDS and other government contractors to build brand awareness, share of the voice in the news media, and market expansion.

Getting the NMCI press release out the door, coordinating multiple sources of information, and getting the OK from "reviewers" and "approvers" were other eye-openers in my transition from the government back to the private sector. From that point, I began to appreciate the confluence of strategies to position government contractors for growth in an increasingly competitive market.

PR is just one tool to reach customers, influencers and ultimately, federal decision-makers who sit in rooms reading responses to Requests for

Proposal, or RFP, issued by agencies awarding contracts to companies to deliver mission-oriented services. What I appreciated from my years leading PR at EDS was the importance of coordinated strategies: marketing, branding, IR, government relations and later, social media, and how they shape the image and brand of companies in the eyes of federal agencies — and ultimately, to build trust.

Building trust between a government contractor and an agency became even more critical when the unthinkable happened. A sunny Tuesday morning in early September forever shook our lives, country, world, and the GovCon industry. On Sep. 11, 2001, I was working from home — which was unusual back then — about to head to D.C. for a meeting at the Federal Aviation Administration. EDS had a long relationship with the FAA and had recently won a new contract we were announcing the next day at a press conference.

I called my contact at the FAA public affairs office around 8:45 a.m. to confirm our meeting later that morning. The call rang and rang. I tried again. *That's odd,* I thought. *Why is no one answering the phone?* Finally, the guy I was supposed to meet answered. "Eileen, I'm sorry, but I can't talk to you right now. Turn on your TV and you'll know what I mean." Click.

As I scurried around my townhouse that morning, getting ready to head into D.C., I didn't know what had happened in lower Manhattan a few minutes earlier. I clicked on the TV in my bedroom. I started watching coverage on CNN of smoke billowing from the World Trade Center. *What the heck?* A few minutes later, the cameras panned to a plane in the sky, flying directly to the second tower.

Boom.

My heart began pounding, and I immediately thought of my brother, Brian, who lived in Brooklyn, and the family of my then-boyfriend (now husband), Andy. A few minutes later, a loud thud shook the windows of my townhouse when the third plane hit the Pentagon, less than 5 miles away from my home. My heart was racing. *Where was Kyle?*

I immediately called his dad, who had custody of Kyle the evening before. He said he had just dropped Kyle off at preschool a few miles away. I then called the school and spoke to the director. Kyle was safe, but no one could leave. For fear of other attacks, they were in lockdown. Everyone was frozen in place. My eyes were glued to CNN.

I'll never forget a conversation I had that afternoon with Gen. Albert "Al" Edmonds, president of EDS Federal. He was a highly respected retired Black U.S. Air Force lieutenant general and former director of the Defense Information Systems Agency. While he wasn't my direct boss, and we hadn't yet worked closely together, he reached me on my cell and asked how I was doing and if my family was OK. I was touched by his outreach. I told him as far as I knew, everyone was alright, and that I had finally tracked down Brian, who made his journey home by walking across the Manhattan Bridge along with thousands of other New Yorkers. Thankfully, Andy's brothers who were officers in the New York City Police Department, were also safe.

"Eileen, we have people at the Pentagon," he said." We're trying to figure out who was there, and if… they're alive." Gen. Edmonds' voice cracked. He was genuinely shaken. "I am putting together a crisis communications team," he said. "Can you get to the office early tomorrow morning? I need you."

From that moment, I came to understand the important relationship between government contractors and the government. Large federal agencies, such as the Department of Defense and the Department of the Navy, rely on contractors for people, scale, security, capacity, and support. Trust is the most important factor in this relationship. My experience in politics and the federal government prepared me for navigating this new and uncertain post-9/11 world.

Despite my initial doubts and uncertainty about getting into the GovCon business, I was becoming more confident in my leadership capabilities and the strategies I brought to solve complex new challenges I'd never seen or experienced before.

CHAPTER 2

TO BE A SUCCESSFUL COMMUNICATIONS LEADER, YOU'VE GOT TO LEARN THE BUSINESS

The days, weeks, and months following 9/11 were a blur. Every day, we learned something new about the terrorist attacks in New York City and on the Pentagon. Then, we heard stories about the brave men and women who diverted Flight 93 from crashing into the nation's capital who died 240 miles away in Shanksville, Pennsylvania.

As our country reeled from an unspeakable tragedy, I worked alongside EDS leadership in a capacity beyond PR. I helped stand up a "war room," where we huddled every morning to share the latest updates from our employees, several who unfortunately perished at the Pentagon. I wrote daily updates for HR and corporate communications leadership to help them understand how we were helping affected employees and their families. I helped our company leadership understand how we supported our customers in a time of grave need. I also helped communicate how we were positioning the company to help our customers adapt, survive, and continue operating in a frightening new era.

Alongside the marketing and business development teams, I created presentations and brochures to describe the capabilities and services we could provide federal agencies in a post-9/11 world. The client teams were hounded by their customers to provide capability statements in new areas such as data security, network security and biometrics. The business development teams worked in overdrive to create new "offerings" to help government agencies respond to new needs and requirements.

During that time, I developed strategies for marketing to the federal government and created my first integrated communications and marketing plan. While I had studied marketing in business school, I hadn't yet been in a role where I had to *actually develop and execute* a marketing strategy.

After 9/11, government agencies were scrambling for help in security and cybersecurity. In January 2002, according to the Pew Research Center, Americans said defending the country from future terrorist attacks was a top priority for the president and Congress. A year after the attacks, the Department of Homeland Security was created to coordinate national security efforts, combining 22 federal departments and agencies into a unified, integrated cabinet-level agency.

It was then I learned about something called "thought leadership." Conferences and seminars sponsored by think tanks and policy institutes were suddenly everywhere. They were looking for former "govies" — as former and current government officials are called — to speak, pontificate, and offer perspectives on how 9/11 happened and what can be done to protect our country from future terrorist threats.

In addition to creating a new slate of products and services, government contractors like EDS were positioning their executives as thought leaders to speak at conferences and give media interviews. Becoming a "talking head" helped government contractors differentiate themselves by promoting their former government officials as experts in areas of vital need such as homeland security, national defense, cybersecurity, and intelligence.

My first foray into the thought leadership and trade show worlds was shortly after 9/11. COMDEX was one of the largest trade shows in the world at the time held every November in Las Vegas. (The last COMDEX show was in 2003.) In 2001, COMDEX focused on "the technology used to enhance security, whether at airports, in office buildings, or on computer networks." EDS already planned to be an exhibitor, but we knew a good way for our brand to stand out was to position our executives as thought leaders in national and homeland security. Getting a speaking gig at COMDEX became a key priority.

Unfortunately, all the major slots were already taken. Industry titans like Microsoft Chairman Bill Gates, Oracle Chairman and CEO Larry Ellison and Cisco Systems President and CEO John Chambers were the headliners.

During a COMDEX planning call, I threw out an idea. "Why don't we create our own speaking event?" I asked. "That way, we can attract people to come to our booth, hear what we have to say, engage with them, and then show them what we do." Although I didn't have much exposure to industry trade shows, I figured it was an opportunity to bring fresh approaches to what felt like a pretty stale and traditional format.

At the time, creating a homegrown speaking event at an exhibit booth wasn't a common practice, I knew getting eyeballs and ears at a crowded trade show required creative thinking.

EDS Federal's President Gen. Edmonds was the obvious choice to speak at COMDEX that year. I worked with him to put together a deck he used to share his perspectives on the war on terror and how EDS could help government agencies adapt and prepare for a post-9/11 world. People lined up to hear Gen. Edmonds. His presentation at the EDS booth was a huge success.

As we traveled back and forth to Las Vegas, Gen. Edmonds shared insights into how an accomplished Air Force and DOD executive approached leadership in the private sector. He was one of my first industry mentors, and I'll never forget his sage advice: "Eileen, in order for you to be a successful communicator, you're going to need to learn the business." I shared with him the conversation I had with Bill Ritz, who said he could teach me IT and GovCon, but not PR. Gen. Edmonds chuckled and spoke in a voice I can still remember. "Yes, I can teach you all of that, but you really need to get inside the business," he said. "Then, you'll be invaluable."

About a year later, thanks to Gen. Edmonds' insistence, I was drafted by the company's education team. It was tasked with delivering on contracts with the Education Department and Federal Student Aid and winning new business with the agency. I segued into a business development role, working alongside professional BD people.

Prior to EDS, I didn't know much about this activity. It was hard to imagine how anyone wanted to write proposals and responses to RFPs for a living. I quickly learned this was an essential part of knowing the business.

I was paired up with some serious BD professionals, including Bill McGovern, who were experts at developing strategies to "capture" new contracts with federal agencies — all day long. I was a decent writer but writing in "proposal speak" was an entirely different style I initially struggled with. Understanding the technical requirements, determining the quantity and types of FTEs — or full-time equivalents — the people needed to work on a particular program or contract — as well as developing the financial estimate — or costs — to submit a competitive bid — was a lot to learn.

I soon figured out this wasn't a role or a job I wanted to do full-time. However, I gained a profound respect for the people who did and were good at it. The good BDers were quickly snatched up by the executives and they held onto them tightly. The good BDers knew their intrinsic value to the business team and made it known which RFPs they'd work on and which ones they could pass onto more junior BDers. I grew to understand the financial incentives for writing a winning proposal and how a BDer's worth was measured in the number of new business proposals won and lost.

During that time, I became more aware of the "business of education" and how a company like EDS partnered with federal agencies like the Education Department and FSA to support their mission and service student borrowers. Many of my colleagues had double badges. That meant they could walk in and out of the Education Department like a federal official. That concept intrigued me. I hadn't come across many contractors while working in the federal government. I began realizing how valuable the people with double badges were to our business.

The concept of "walking the hallways" often came up during our team calls. "Who's been walking the halls?" was a routine question by the executives. "Yup, I walked the halls the other day" was a typical response and an answer that seemed to resonate well with the execs. As long as our BD team members performed this function, or at least said they were, they were held in high regard as it supposedly demonstrated they knew how to talk to our customers and find new opportunities to pursue. Getting inside intelligence directly from a customer about a new business opportunity was like liquid gold. Whether they got anything of value was always a head-scratcher for me.

While I had been out of the administration for about two years, I still had a political bug. Mark Warner, a well-known business leader who lives in Alexandria, Virginia, founded a venture capital firm that invested in cellular technology including Nextel. Mark ran for governor of Virginia and was elected in 2001. As a fellow resident of Alexandria, I was excited to see him get elected. On a whim, I checked out state committees looking for people to serve. I applied to the secretary of the commonwealth to serve on the Virginia Business Education Partnership.

Honestly, I had no idea what this partnership did, but I thought I could bring valuable perspectives from my work at EDS and my years in politics during the Clinton administration. I was elated when I was accepted to serve for a two-year term starting July 1, 2002.

It was a thrill to get back in the mix and experience politics at the state level, which I hadn't yet done. I told my manager about my appointment, and she didn't seem too impressed. I said I'd make sure my work on the partnership didn't conflict with my job and perhaps I might pick up some good intelligence about new business opportunities for EDS, which interested her a bit more.

My role with the partnership opened my eyes to a whole new world of state politics. Every three months or so, I traveled to Richmond and met with members of the partnership to review grant applications for organizations and businesses partnering with Virginia-area schools, colleges, and universities. It was fascinating to learn about the relationships between companies and educational institutions that relied on outside resources to support their programs. As Kyle was about to enter kindergarten, I grew curious to learn more about how education was funded, who made policy and decided what our kids would learn in the classroom.

Around that time, the proposal I'd been working on for a good part of six months was successfully awarded to EDS and three other companies. It was the first time I'd worked on a winning proposal, and it was exhilarating.

Back then, this was the largest contract awarded by the Education Department and another crown jewel in the GovCon space. It was a keystone project for FSA called Common Services for Borrowers. The prime contractor, the former ACS, oversaw integrating the other companies including EDS, Raytheon and Pearson Government Solutions, a division of Pearson, the U.K.-based media and education company.

The goal of the CSB program, as outlined by the Education Department, was to modernize and integrate four separate legacy systems into one Performance-Based Contract. Collectively, these systems serviced almost 9 million student borrowers at the time. And they were run by four different companies.

Little did I know, the lead EDS executive bid me to work on the new contract as the lead communications manager to liaise with FSA's communications office. When I learned more details, I was excited as it'd take me back into the government in a familiar role. Plus, my commute to D.C. was a heck of a lot better than trucking out to Herndon every day.

As a student who needed loans to get through undergraduate and business school, I had no idea there were so many disparate systems that required so many outside companies to support an agency like FSA. That was my starting point to begin thinking of creative yet straightforward ways to communicate the impact we'd help make.

I sat through countless meetings and conference calls, listening to all the mumbo jumbo. I wanted to find a way to communicate in plain English how our efforts would impact our customer and their customers: student borrowers. For example, how would we make the whole process easier? Would we save them time? How could their experience be better? How could we save FSA and the Education Department money? And how could we help our customer communicate to its stakeholders — Congress, student borrowers, advocacy groups, lenders, schools — how these "common services" were *actually* making things better?

Pressing for answers was a lot harder than I imagined. As much of a nudge I became, I realized that was the job of a communicator. And it was also part of knowing the business. Being the one to connect the dots and ask the hard questions to get the answers I needed became my edge, which I brought to future challenges.

Little did I know then the next big challenge was right around the corner.

CHAPTER 3

A CRISIS IS A TERRIBLE THING TO WASTE

As a child, moving from Milwaukee to Rochester was a hugely influential event. Being uprooted from a familiar environment and thrust into the unknown taught me resilience and adaptability, two traits that became core to who I'm as a professional today. In those early days, I had to quickly learn what it takes to come to a new place and find my bearings. At 10, I found myself in a completely different city, somewhat anxiety-ridden and nervous, thinking I'd never see my place in this new world or find my path.

Those feelings were similar to what I felt leading communications for this significant contract with the Education Department. It was a daily challenge to coordinate updates, reports, and presentations. In any given week, we had multiple calls and meetings to update the customer. Many times, I looked around the room to gauge the expressions on their faces. I got to know some of the customers and sensed when they weren't fully grasping our GovCon "project speak."

Having been on their side of the aisle, I knew what they needed: simple and straightforward information.

Getting to the heart of the tangible progress we were making versus what felt like a lot of churn was a relentless quest. I pushed — sometimes to the point of annoyance — to understand the status of a project, percentage of completion, and if there were any risks to address or mitigate. Staying on top of it all not only stretched my management capabilities but certainly my patience.

During that time, I got to know our teaming partners. Until that point, I pretty much worked with fellow EDS colleagues. As I was interacting with so many different people, there were moments when I'd ask someone, "So, which company are you with?" While I grew to understand it was the role of the prime contractor to bring together the greater team and ensure seamless integration of resources, I still was trying to figure out who was who and whom to go to for what.

As the project picked up steam, we needed more room beyond the offices we had at FSA headquarters inside the CNN building in Northeast D.C., behind Union Station. Somehow, I got roped into scouting out possible space and developing requirements that could accommodate several hundred people. I took a trip to Gaithersburg, Maryland, nearly 30 miles from downtown D.C., to look at a vacant building. I had lived in the D.C. area for most of my life and knew the region well from visiting my relatives in suburban Maryland, I couldn't imagine that location was convenient for our customer in D.C. and most of the team who lived in Northern Virginia.

For reasons I'll never fully understand, we picked that building in Gaithersburg off Interstate 270 North. Soon after, the teams settled into a new place that felt like the other side of the moon.

In a few short months, we outgrew our new digs. Every office, cubicle, and conference room were packed to the gills. As a people manager, I needed to develop a schedule so our staff could book rooms and offices in advance. If you didn't have a team meeting or needed a conference room, you were encouraged to work at another location. It was a constant scramble to find a desk and a chair and the necessary conference call "squawk box."

I often had to let my team use my office and float around with my laptop and find empty conference rooms or other locations. I'll never forget a drive I made one morning to Gaithersburg, which was a good hour commute in heavy traffic from my home in Alexandria. I had back-to-back meetings and calls scheduled. When I arrived, not only was my office busy; there wasn't one empty chair or desk in the entire building. With tears in my eyes, I walked out to my car and set up the office in my front seat. I remember looking in the rear-view mirror, with tears rolling down my cheeks, and saying, *This whole shtick was starting to get real old.*

One of the people I got to know during this time was Judy Martin, who worked with Pearson Government Solutions, one of the subcontractors on the CSB contract. Judy, who was from Iowa, was a gem and one of those rare people who wasn't only knowledgeable and helpful but also extremely nice.

Occasionally, we met for coffee and talked about our families and the challenges on the project. Out of the blue, Judy asked if she could share my resume with the CEO of Pearson Government Solutions. Judy had heard he was looking for a vice president of communications. Was I interested? I was flattered that a colleague considered me for a role that would push my boundaries and propel me into the executive ranks.

I grew increasingly frustrated with the Gaithersburg commute. I remember during a major snowstorm, my car died on 270 North on my way to the office. The whole situation made me feel a bit like a hamster in a hamster wheel. I vented to my immediate manager about feeling mismatched with my newest responsibilities, but she didn't seem to care too much.

I decided to go for the opportunity at Pearson.

It was during that time I married Andy. We tied the knot on April 24, 2004, and brought together our families. It was one of the happiest days of my life. Through our marriage, my son, Kyle, then 6, gained a stepbrother, Drew, 8, at the time. We bought a beautiful house in the Del Ray neighborhood of Alexandria and started a new life together. Andy encouraged me to explore new opportunities and supported my desire to get into a different role that would allow me to continue growing professionally.

Soon after, I interviewed with Pearson Government Solutions President and CEO Mac Curtis, one of the GovCon industry's titans. Over breakfasts and lunches, I met with his executive team. I seized the opportunity to pick their brains about what and whom they were looking for. In my final interview, Mac asked if I could draw up a plan to outline my first 90 days and approaches to crisis communications and media relations. That question piqued my interest. We talked about the company's challenges with a contract it won with the recently formed Transportation Security Administration. He told me about a prominent senator who had gone on national TV to excoriate Pearson for "wasting taxpayers' money by recruiting screeners at luxury resorts."

Apparently, CNN cameras showed up at the office unannounced to demand answers. Mac said the company did its best to handle the situation.

"Holy crap," I said to myself.

I shared with Mac my experiences with crisis communications and media relations, drawing on my time at EDS and in government. In some ways, creating that plan felt like free consulting. Still, I knew I had to put in writing how I'd bring together varying views and opinions of what Mac and the leadership team thought a communications leader should do to chart a new course and build a new communications function. It was the ultimate test.

When I got the call that I got the job, I was elated. I gave notice at EDS and used my exit interview to share feedback with leadership about the last couple years of my tenure. Going from the head of PR for the federal business to what felt like a gopher plugging the holes of weak management wasn't the best fit for me and it certainly wasn't the best use of my time. As much as I hoped I could have continued building my career in a company that gave me my first taste of GovCon, it was time to spread my wings. And I was ready for a new challenge.

Things started out promising. Going to my new office at Pearson Government Solutions in the Ballston neighborhood of Arlington was a hop, skip, and jump compared to the horrendous commutes I had at EDS. As I settled into being married again and raising my son and stepson, working closer to home was a welcome change.

My first day at Pearson was surreal. Mac asked a wonderful young woman, Trang Phan (now Mar), to work with me. A recent Penn State graduate, Trang was excited and eager to learn more about communications and PR. I was excited to partner with such a bright, warm, and talented professional who'd help me learn about the company and introduce me to folks around the business.

But nothing prepared me for my second day on the job. As I was organizing my new office and situating my desk that morning, I heard a tap at my door. As I looked up, I saw two men standing in front of me.

"Hello, can I help you? And who are you?" I asked them.

"We certainly hope so. I'm Robert O'Harrow and this is Scott Higham. We're investigative reporters with The Washington Post. Mac told us about you. Do you have a few minutes?"

Gulp.

My first instinct was to ask: How the heck did you get past the front desk? And how did you find my office? At that point, it didn't matter. I couldn't do anything about it. These reporters weren't leaving until they got what they needed. And now, I had to figure out what to tell them — and prove to Mac he made the right choice in hiring me to manage what became the ultimate test in strength, resilience, fortitude, judgment, skill, and crisis communications over the next six months.

As I sat there, staring these two reporters in the eyes, I tried to maintain at least a façade of calm and composure. I knew how to deal with an ambush. I just needed more information, which required me to buy some time. If you've dealt with reporters, you know time is the first thing you negotiate before agreeing to any terms or before providing any information.

"What's your deadline?" is the first question you ask. I learned that during my years at Hill+Knowlton.

"So, Mr. O'Harrow and Mr. Higham, what's your deadline?

"Eileen, please call us Robert and Scott. And our deadline is Thursday, in two days. We've already got the first story ready to go. It'll be in Sunday's paper. Frontpage, above the fold. All we're waiting on is your statement."

Gulp. Frontpage. Above the fold. First story?

I invited them into my office to sit down and have a conversation. Over the next half hour, they told me about an audit report they got from a trusted anonymous source that showed how Pearson made questionable spending decisions that resulted in the TSA contract rising from $104 million to more than $740 million. They'd include how much the company spent on Starbucks coffee, the cost to rent extension cords, phone calls, and hotel elevator operators — those kinds of frontpage sensationalistic stories we've all read in The Post.

"The high cost of a rush to security, that's what we're writing about," said Robert and Scott. "Pearson jacked up the cost of the contract. Pearson took advantage of 9/11."

Say what? I thought. *How could that be?* The only way Pearson could have changed the contract is if the customer greenlighted that. Every modification to a government contract requires a government-approved change order.

"I'll get back to you. Now, let me walk you out."

Over the next 48 hours, I got a crash course in the contract Pearson was competitively awarded three years earlier to recruit and screen the federal airport security force for the newly created TSA. The task was to assist TSA in the wake of the 9/11 terrorist attacks and mobilize the largest government workforce since World War II. More than 130,000 prospective employees had to be vetted and screened to deploy the new security system at every airport in every state — within a timeframe Congress set that was highly ambitious under the best of circumstances.

TSA awarded the contract to Pearson because of its nationwide network of 925 assessment centers and experience in testing large numbers of individuals in those centers. Pearson's proposal was to send TSA recruits to Pearson-run assessment centers and to other facilities for medical and security evaluations. By using existing networks, Pearson could efficiently reach the goals and deadlines of the contract — and save the government a lot of money. However, after TSA awarded Pearson the contract, the agency changed the requirements. It decided to use a different model that would establish assessment centers within a specified distance from approximately 429 commercial airports nationwide.

This entailed renting a hotel or similar space at the going local rates. In many cases, such as near resorts, the only available facilities that met the TSA requirements for timing, size, security, and proximity were very expensive. Few of these resorts offered discounts on anything from coffee to telephones. Hiring temporary employees to manage the operations at these locations was also tricky. The list of logistical challenges was enormous.

But Pearson rolled up its sleeves and went to work. It met all deadlines and successfully helped TSA install a federal force of security screeners nationwide in record time.

Adm. James Loy, then-undersecretary of transportation, said, "In a time of national urgency, five months after 9/11, Pearson stepped up to the plate and helped make our airports and air travel more secure." It was, he said, "Nothing short of a major and historical accomplishment."

As I learned about TSA's decision to change the model for where the assessment centers would be located, I knew I needed to dig more. After all, it was the government's decision to take a different approach — not Pearson's. That Pearson was operating as directed by TSA didn't seem to matter.

But I knew — it did matter.

That's what I needed to find out and explain to these hungry and determined reporters. And I thought to myself, *I'd be damned if they earn a Pulitzer from these stories!*

The two reporters who showed up in front of my office were clearly interested in more than just "your average Washington story." They wanted a multi-faceted and contentious series of stories that gave them something to write about for months. "Guilty until proven innocent" seemed to be their approach. They had already decided Pearson was responsible for the high-cost overruns, believing Pearson had manipulated the changes that led to the use of expensive hotels and facilities instead of the cheaper assessment centers. They weren't interested in hearing any evidence that contradicted their mistaken belief.

To these two reporters, their "liquid gold" was a leaked confidential draft audit report from the Defense Contract Audit Agency, which they planned to use as an outline for their first frontpage story.

After poring through boxes of files with Mac and a legion of lawyers and PR agencies we quickly lined up, we had to somehow convince these reporters the draft audit in their hot little hands was inaccurate and misleading.

I quickly realized these reporters writing about an alleged high cost of a rush to security were rushing to publish front-page stories riddled with inaccuracies and omitting important facts. *The irony,* I thought. They kept trying to play this game of giving me no time to respond. I knew their one-sided questions about decisions and documents filed three years earlier required research to provide thoughtful statements and rebuttals. I kept pushing back and demanded more time. It started to work. I thought *A crisis is a terrible thing to waste.*

This was my moment.

When The Post refused to print our response submitted in a letter-to-the-editor, it revealed the paper's editorial stance and gave the reporters the green light to pursue more stories. As they pressed for more details, information, and juicy tidbits, I changed our approach.

After weeks of bad press and feeling like things couldn't get any worse, I stood up to the journalists' pressure by refusing their demands for a quick turnaround and demanding they come to our offices for a background conversation before giving them any more information. This allowed us to better understand what they wanted and what documents we needed to refute their accusations.

After a series of face-to-face meetings with Mac and other senior executives who led the TSA project, the reporters began to hear a different story. This story made them scratch their heads and wonder what had really gone on inside TSA. Maybe, they came to understand Pearson had been telling them the truth all along. It took hours to walk through countless documents and reports that clearly showed Pearson informed TSA from the beginning of the contract that its decision would cost nearly $700 million more to implement. In essence, we gave these reporters a crash course in how the federal government manages contracts.

One day, I took a taxi to TSA's headquarters across the street from Pentagon City Mall. Mark Hatfield, Jr., son of the late Sen. Mark Hatfield of Oregon, led public affairs for the new agency. From my years in politics,

I knew he had a significant role in communicating with the news media and could help tell a complete and more accurate story.

I reached out to Mark over the phone and told him Pearson was getting annihilated in the news media. I asked him if he could approve a joint statement about TSA's decision to change the requirements of the contract it awarded to Pearson. He asked me to draft something and show it to him. As I sat across from him in his office as he read it, he looked up at me and said, "I'm sorry, but I can't sign off on this." I asked if I could rework the statement or tone it down, but he basically said nothing. I knew then I wasn't getting anywhere, but I was proud that I tried.

When it came time to publish what the reporters said was their last story on the TSA contract, I knew our more aggressive approach had turned the tide. It took almost three years to prove the increased contract decisions were actually directed by TSA, and this was what changed the whole project approach and cost. Eventually, the reporters acknowledged this in their final story and exonerated Pearson while blaming TSA for the cost overruns.

And that last story would have made the first page, above the fold, if it weren't for a major earthquake in Turkey that bumped it to the back pages of the A section of The Post.

It's hard to remember much else during those months of my life. With the support of my family and great teamwork at the office, I somehow got through it — and lived to tell about it.

Looking back, my experience taught me important lessons about what to anticipate when working on a large, high-profile government contract and how to ready oneself for the scrutiny and demands that often accompany such work. Overall, this experience made me a stronger and more resilient communicator.

Over the next year, when the dust somewhat settled, I documented my experience in a case study with the help of Don Goldberg at our PR agency, Qorvis. (Don went on to form Bluetext, a leading digital marketing agency). I presented it at events and published blogs and articles. It was amazing — and therapeutic — to see how much my experience resonated with fellow PR practitioners. I essentially boiled down my lessons learned into three key points I continue to live by:

Stay on message, even if no one is listening. Before sitting down with reporters, develop key talking points and messages. In every interview, conversation, and phone call, repeat these messages over and over again, even if they' aren't listening. Eventually, those messages penetrate and change the dialogue.

Demand more time and wave a carrot to get them to agree. Don't be intimidated by unrealistic deadlines and scare tactics reporters often use to get you to say what they want you to say. If you know you have information that'll get their attention, tell them, and they'll find ways to push their deadlines.

From the start, set the tone for how you expect to be treated. Don't let reporters treat you like you're their lackey. If you let them abuse you the first time, they'll keep treating you the same. Demand respect by establishing ground rules — and stick to your commitments. Reporters will eventually figure out they can't mess with you.

CHAPTER 4

REBRAND? NO PROBLEM.

Not long after the TSA/Post ordeal, I learned "Mother Pearson" — as we affectionately called the company — was spinning off the government services business. Honestly, it didn't shock me. The scrutiny from The Post's TSA investigation undoubtedly took a toll on Pearson's brand and reputation. In a few months, we'd become a "stand-alone entity" owned by a private equity firm. And we needed a new name ASAP.

If you have gone through a spinoff and a rebrand, you know it's a gigantic headache. A friend said she'd rather get a root canal than do a rebrand. At the time, the only experience I had with rebranding was while I was in the Clinton administration. During my tenure at the U.S. and Foreign Commercial Service, which is part of the International Trade Administration at the Commerce Department, we successfully rebranded to a simpler name, The Commercial Service. Over many months, we developed a new identity and a refreshed logo still used today. It's an accomplishment I've always been proud of.

While not an apples-to-apples comparison, I used that experience to develop a strategy to extricate Pearson's government services business from "the mothership" and develop a new name, identity, and brand to propel it to success as a stand-alone business. It would be a massive lift without the marketing, IT, HR, and infrastructure support tethered to an established global corporation. The transition required all hands on deck to meet a multitude of concurrent requests, deadlines, and timeframes coming from different directions.

One morning, Mac came into my office. He said we needed a new name to replace Pearson Government Solutions in two weeks to insert into documents drawn up by the private equity firm Veritas Capital.

Wait a minute, two weeks?

It felt like a huge weight was thrown on my shoulders. I recalled the many months it took while I was at the Commerce Department to get a new name and logo created, vetted, and ultimately approved. We didn't have months, Mac reminded me. We had 14 days.

"How hard can it be?" was a typical response I'd get from colleagues. "Make one up! That's what Accenture did!" was another reaction.

I did some research and learned how Accenture came up with its iconic name in early 2001 through an employee contest that took more than 80 days. It was chosen from a pool of 5,000 different names. Wow, 5,000 names? That seemed unreal to me. *Okay,* I thought *I could do the same thing.* But I didn't have 80 days! I knew the company had many smart people. But what if we can't come up with a decent name in two weeks? That couldn't be the *only* strategy.

I challenged employees to think of a new name that captured the history and future direction of the business. "Help us come up with a new name that embodies our business' unique history, vision, and mission as we move into the next chapter as a premier government contractor" was the prompt I sent to over 5,000 employees.

To that point, we were known as the government contractor that could design, build, and operate solutions to deliver mission-critical services to our customers with the people, processes, and technology behind the scenes making it all possible. "Be creative. Think outside the box. But remember, the name can't already be taken, and we'll need to find a unique URL," I told employees.

First new name strategy, check.

Second new name strategy: Get a good branding agency.

When I called a few Madison Avenue advertising agencies to ask for their help, they laughed when I said I needed a new name in two weeks with the parameters of a minuscule budget. I found one agency willing to crank out some names, but it couldn't make any promises. I knew I needed a Plan B and thought, *nothing beats raw ingenuity.*

That week, after Andy and I put our kids to bed, we sat in our living room with our laptops, searching and brainstorming for new names until the wee hours of the morning. It was equal parts hilarious, crazy, frustrating, exhausting, and nerve-wracking. We kept finding good names, then discovered they were already taken. I kept thinking, *Now I know why those ad agencies make the big bucks.*

As the clock was ticking, I knew we'd have to settle on a new name soon. I had a whiteboard in my office where coworkers randomly came in and wrote suggestions. I'd come back from a meeting or from lunch and find smiley faces next to ridiculous names that gave me a chuckle or two. A little levity kept things in perspective.

Every couple of days, Mac asked me for the status of the top names. I gave him a running list and told him I was still checking trademarks and URLs. I knew we needed a name with a dot-com, which was a major challenge.

One day, I got an email from an employee with a suggestion: Vangent. *What the heck kind of name was that?* The employee said it was like Accenture's name, derived from "accent on the future." "Vangent is kind of like that, it's a combination of 'vanguard' and 'cogent,'" he said. *Hmmm. That's interesting.* "We're leading the way to cogent ideas" was the thinking behind it. It took a while to wrap my head around Vangent, let alone pronounce it. But it quickly rose to the top of the list.

One employee said it sounded like a feminine product.

But by far, Vangent had the greatest potential.

The only problem? The Van Gent family in the Netherlands owned vangent.com. I remember saying to my colleagues: "Have you heard of Van Gogh? Well, it's close to Van Gent. Maybe they're neighbors?" When we landed on the name, we hadn't thought it was someone's actual family name. The timing was tight, so we used a domain service to negotiate an offer. I don't recall how much we offered, but it wasn't that much. I'll never forget the night before the name had to be finalized. We were waiting until 3 or 4 a.m. for a response — and it was a miracle when they accepted our offer.

Bingo. It happened. We were going to be called Vangent.

The ensuing months were a bit of a blur as things started moving extremely fast. I started to engage PR agencies to meet a flurry of deadlines. We needed to get everything rebranded and create a variety of new assets, including a new website. I was blessed to have met Jaime O'Keefe (now Orlando), who worked for a PR agency at the time. A gifted communicator who approaches challenges and opportunities in a thoughtful and nonconventional way, Jaime quickly became my right hand. She helped create a brand playbook to explain the meaning of the new brand, which was sent to all employees. It was a huge hit.

On top of all the activity at work, I was expecting my second child. I sat in my office when my doctor called with the results of the CVS test — chorionic villus sampling — which is a prenatal screening used to detect birth defects, genetic diseases, and other problems during pregnancy. I was considered "advanced maternal age," so when the doctor said everything looked good and we were having a girl, I started bawling tears of joy. Kyle and Drew would soon have a baby sister. My dream of building our family was coming true.

During this time, another dynamic entered my life. One night, I got a call from Rob Krupicka, then a member of the Alexandria City Council, who encouraged me to run for the school board. As I had lived in Alexandria for about 10 years, I started to get to know some of the elected officials by being involved with Kyle's school, the Parent Teachers Association, and the local civic association. An election was coming up in May and all three school board positions in my district were open.

"Eileen, you're a great communicator," Rob said to me. "You can help our schools by serving on the school board."

"Are you kidding me?" I recall saying. I was working full time, managing a rebrand, raising my kids, and expecting my second child. Where on Earth would I find the time to run to the office? What's the expression — if you want something done, ask a busy person to do it?

At first, I couldn't fathom taking on a campaign to run for office. Andy and I had many conversations about how we'd manage. We went back and forth. He knew I had an itch to run for the office. The question that kept bubbling to the surface: *Could I actually win this race*? I relied on Andy's judgment; after all, he was a community organizer in New York City, where he grew up and was a lead member of Vice President Al Gore's advance team when they won the White House in 1992. He has great political instincts and understands political dynamics better than anyone I know.

After we did the analysis, I decided to throw my hat in the ring, at the last minute. To pull it off, I needed a lot of help. I first called my brother, Brian, a gifted web designer, and asked if he could build a website for my campaign. I then called our wedding photographer and asked him to take my headshot. Andy started to schedule meetings with education experts he knew from the Clinton administration, who advised me on issues to focus my campaign.

As Andy was a full-time attorney at the Advancement Project, a well-known and respected social justice organization, he didn't have time to run my campaign. He reached out to his friend, Charlie Ramos, a community organizer from the Bronx and talked him into becoming my campaign manager. Charlie had a great network of political organizers enthusiastic about helping me get elected to the Alexandria City School board and become a voice for the Latino population.

Soon after, I contacted teachers and administrators at Kyle's school and the school system to better understand immigrant children's needs inside the classrooms. I also met with leaders of local immigrant organizations about their challenges working with the schools. Being fluent in Spanish, I saw an opportunity to become the voice for our city's large Latino immigrant population who needed an advocate and help their kids do better in school.

As I gathered more data about the widening achievement gap in our school system — a disparity in academic achievement and educational performance between minority and disadvantaged students, and their white counterparts — I got more fired up about my decision to run.

Things started to click, and it began to feel like a calling. I was unlocking a new purpose in my life and using my God-given talents to lead, communicate, represent, and make a difference.

Just about every day when I came home from work, Andy said, "OK, sweetie, get on your walking shoes. We're knocking on doors." It didn't matter how exhausted I was or how much I wanted to chill out and take a break. Going door to door was the only way I could engage and meet people and ask them to vote for me. I'd grab my stack of campaign flyers, a Sharpie, and a big jug of water and we'd spend two to three hours walking door to door in different neighborhoods across the city.

Between canvassing, we'd come home and make sure the kids were safe, doing their homework, and had dinner on the table. Friends and relatives joined me in doing GOTV — Get Out the Vote — to introduce myself to voters, talk to them about their concerns, and tell them why I was running for the school board.

Nearing my final trimester, I was visibly pregnant and got some interesting looks from people. "So, you're running for office while you're expecting?" they asked. I chuckled and said, "Yup, I know I'm crazy, but I know I can make a difference for our students, teachers, and schools."

With the knowledge and perspectives I gained from the hundreds of conversations going door to door in my community, the picture started to crystallize in my mind. I saw myself as that representative, connector, and advocate for parents and families to help them navigate our school system, represent their needs, and champion their interests.

There were moments when I got so excited about the prospects of doing this kind of work that was so different from my "day job" at Vangent. *If I get elected, how on Earth am I going to juggle working full time, take care of my baby, raise my sons, and serve in elected office?* I thought.

I kept reminding myself I wasn't doing this for the money. School board members earned $15,000 a year, which just about covered the cost of commuting to school board meetings and paying for babysitters, after taxes. And I wasn't doing it because it was the best time to run for office. I was doing it because the stars were aligning. It felt like an outer body force propelled and pushed me every day with energy and determination I never knew I had.

That "one more thing" started to feel like a new dimension in my life meant to happen, to round out who I was and whom I wanted to become.

Mostly, I kept my school board campaign on the "Q.T" at the office and maintained a healthy distance between my day job and what became my new night and weekend job.

After we landed on Vangent as the new name, my rebranding plans started coming together. Thanks to my talented team and the outside marketing and ad agencies I brought on to develop a new messaging platform and website, I kept things moving. Yes, there were absolute moments of panic, mainly driven by nights when I barely slept a few hours. Somehow, I kept my composure on the work and home fronts because of Andy and my family's incredible patience and support.

To my surprise, my school board candidacy picked up steam. I saw traction with good comments about me on social media and positive reviews in local papers. My hot-pink, fluorescent yard signs with "Rivera for School Board" were getting noticed.

Between multiple debates, community forums, op-eds, and ads I wrote and placed in local papers and continuous door-knocking, I gained supporters in what became a close four-way race for three slots in District A of Alexandria, which I was running to represent. We held near nightly meetings on our dining room table as election day approached. We called everyone to work the polls on election day, including my relatives, former coworkers, neighbors, and my mom and dad who flew in from Milwaukee.

Then — it happened. I finished in second place — in the top three — right behind Sheryl Gorsuch, the well-known PTA leader in our community, who became a confidante and a close friend during the campaign and helped me build trust among the city's education "elites."

After the polls closed, I got congratulatory calls from the elected officials. Andy and I got in our car and made our grand entrance at the Alexandria Democratic Party's victory party in Old Town Alexandria.

It felt surreal to waddle into the ballroom with the other electeds, close to 8 months pregnant. Wow, I thought. I managed to get elected to public office while rebranding a company in my last trimester. Now, what would I accomplish next?

CHAPTER 5

KNOW THY AUDIENCE

I was sworn into office exactly a month before giving birth to our daughter, Carmen Jacqueline Rivera, named after her two amazing grandmothers. On that hot summer day, in a light-blue maternity dress with my gigantic pregnant belly sticking out after I held my right hand to take the oath of office, I gave a short speech about what influenced me to run for office.

I dedicated my win to my late grandfather, John "Jack" Fitzgerald Cassidy, who was a city clerk and alderman in Milwaukee, Wisconsin in the 1920's. He was active in Democratic politics and ran for the U.S. Congress to represent the fourth district of Wisconsin in 1938 but came in fourth place in the primary. Today, Congresswoman Gwen Moore represents the fourth district of Wisconsin.

Thaddeus Wasielewski, an attorney in Milwaukee, won the Democratic primary in 1938, but lost in the general election to Republican John Schafer. Paul Gauer, a progressive political leader like Grandpa Jack, was also on the Democratic primary ticket that year. I learned later Gauer was a socialist alderman in the Bay View neighborhood of Milwaukee, where I lived until 1973 when we moved to Rochester, New York. My parents both went to

Bay View High School. Incidentally, my family lived on Gauer Circle, named after him. No wonder progressive politics are in my blood!

While I didn't know my grandfather very well as he passed away when I was 9, my dad told me about his outgoing personality and how he supported his family during the tough times after the Great Depression.

After I took office, Mom and Dad framed one of Grandpa Jack's campaign flyers: "Capable." "Dependable." "For Collective Bargaining for both Employers and Employees." "For Roosevelt Recovery Program." "Advocates 100% Americanism in Our Schools and Colleges." That last line got my attention and spurred me to research and understand what it meant.

After many talks with my dad who shared stories about his dad, I learned more about why Grandpa Jack supported "100% Americanism." "The concept of 100 percent Americanism arose from the founding of The American Legion in 1919 at the end of the first World War to build national pride, advance patriotism, promote U.S. citizenship, educate young people (mentally and physically alike), promote the U.S. Constitution and to counter threats to freedom, democracy, law and order, which the founders had pledged their lives to defend." This description comes from the website of The American Legion, which Congress chartered in 1919 as a "patriotic veterans' organization."

As I dug deeper, I learned this movement came about between the world wars and led to the persecution of thousands of Jehovah's Witnesses and the expulsion of their children from school. That was because they refused to salute the flag, as they don't salute anyone or anything except God, according to the History Channel's website. "What began as a movement to encourage loyalty to a nation with 'liberty and justice for all' had deviated into the suppression of dissent and unquestioning homage to the flag." Wow, what a controversial policy position Grandpa Jack supported!

I remember thinking after taking the oath of office on that hot sunny day in 2006, if only I could have talked to Grandpa Jack to ask him about his position supporting "100 percent Americanism" and why it was an important message for his campaign for Congress.

While he didn't advance past the primary and never pursued elected office again — and instead went on to sell cars — Grandpa Jack stood for something he obviously cared about. And more than likely, so did his constituents. Connecting with an audience over something you care and feel passionate about is a trait I felt I was born with. I finally knew why.

After Carmen was born, I took maternity leave to spend time with her and get accustomed to having a baby again. Although on a break from my day job, my mom duties and school board service were all consuming, but in a good way. Between taking care of Carmen, taking her on walks in our neighborhood, helping the boys get back and forth from school, and managing their activities and homework, I prepared for school board meetings every other Thursday evening and committee meetings in between. The influx of emails from anxious constituents came with questions about school system policies, clarifications of past decisions, or expressions of their position on an agenda item at an upcoming meeting.

I had been warned about the flood of emails and phone calls I'd soon get as a newly elected official and being responsive to constituent inquiries was important to my new role. I did my best to keep on top of all the emails, phone calls, and requests to speak at civic association meetings across the city. It was an exciting yet demanding time of my life. I'll never be able to thank my patient husband and understanding family enough for what they endured during those years.

The old adage about maternity leave never being long enough was true as I had to quickly juggle work, a newborn, raising our sons, and being a newly elected representative in my community.

My boss, Mac, was understanding and patient throughout my maternity leave. He kept me in the loop while I was tackling activities related to the upcoming transaction to make Vangent a stand-alone company. As I returned to the office with my trusty breast pump, I navigated a new life that felt like I had stomped my foot on the accelerator to a constant 95 mph every day.

Between conference calls and meetings, I taped a sign on my office door that said: "The cow needs to be milked, please come back later. Moooo!" I pumped bottles of milk, stored them in my office fridge, and sometimes found time to make a "milk run" back to the house at lunchtime. When my parents visited before they moved to Annapolis, Maryland, my dad met me in front of my building in Arlington, and I handed over bottles of milk, and he brought them home to keep Carmen nourished.

I breastfed Kyle for almost a year and was determined to breastfeed Carmen for at least a year, no matter what it took. My fellow school board member, Sheryl, helped us find an amazing nanny, Sara Flores, who came to our home every morning to take care of Carmen, which allowed me to go back to work. Sara became — and still is — integral to our family. I'll be forever grateful to her.

The transaction that officially decoupled Vangent from Pearson was finalized in early 2007 and kicked off another journey for me as a communications leader. It was my first time being part of a business carved out from a company and "sold" to a private equity firm. Vangent was an investment of the Veritas Capital Equity Fund, and a big portion of the investors were bondholders.

That meant we had to produce a quarterly press release, conduct quarterly calls with the investor community, and file reports with the Securities and Exchange Commission. Even though I was armed with a banking and finance background and an MBA, IR was a whole new responsibility.

The additional role leading IR expanded my horizons in ways I never anticipated. For starters, I gained a new appreciation for the financial "underbelly" of the company and what it takes to successfully run a GovCon business.

I hired two talented communications and marketing professionals, Jan Lamoglia and Jeri Kirschner, who became my extended left and right hands. I also spent a good deal of time with Chief Financial Officer Jim Reagan, a smart, savvy, and well-respected business leader, who taught me what information mattered to investors and finance people.

As I took on the IR role, "know thy audience" was drilled into me. Bondholders are a different breed than other investors like institutional investors or financial analysts, so you must know whom you're communicating with to know what information they want.

As Jim and I strategized about messaging the upcoming quarter, he shared draft financial statements, highlights, and key metrics such as revenue, operating margins, days sales outstanding, earnings before taxes, interest, depreciation and amortization, or EBITDA, and other common performance indicators.

I analyzed the information and asked: "What drove our revenue growth over the last quarter?" or "What impacted a decrease in operating margin, year over year?" He provided good backup, but my job was to find out the key drivers of different directions the business took in any given quarter and understand the historical context and future plans.

From there, I locked myself in my office, grabbed some Diet Cokes, got in front of my computer, and stitched together scripts for Mac and Jim to explain Vangent's financial performance each quarter. It was a ton to learn, master, and pull off every 90 days.

After we got through an earnings call, which required close coordination with a conference call company, I typically had several follow-up calls from investors and the media. Answering questions and framing the narrative for both key audiences required careful planning, preparation, and execution. It was paramount to ensure everyone got the information they needed in a timely way.

And it also was my job to make sure investors and the media alike responded positively through favorable news stories and reports by the analyst community following the company and other government contractors.

Joining the National Investor Relations Institute, known as NIRI, headquartered in Alexandria, Virginia, was a godsend. Over the four-plus years, I led IR at Vangent, I learned from fellow IR professionals who taught me how to succeed in my new profession.

I devoured NIRI's newsletters and participated in as many conference calls and seminars as I could. I attended the organization's annual conference, where I met people like me at companies from around the country. One year, I was on a panel and shared my experiences and lessons leading IR at a GovCon company. I developed relationships with people I've kept in touch with to this day.

I began to really enjoy IR. I contemplated how I could give up media relations, communications and marketing and *just* do IR.

At the time, IR started including the emerging area of corporate social responsibility, which was intriguing to me. I started helping the company think about our contributions to the communities where we worked and where our employees lived. I helped the company formulate strategies to be conscious of our impact and how we could enhance the community and environment. It was really interesting.

As we approached the fifth year of being owned by Veritas Capital, I sensed a change on the horizon. The company had tripled in size from $300 million in revenue to close to $1 billion. Through conversations with Mac and Jim, I learned we were preparing for two scenarios: going public or being acquired by a "strategic" buyer such as a much larger company.

If the first scenario happened, Mac asked what would I want my future role to be following an Initial Public Offering — communications or IR? "IR, of course!" I quickly responded. I continued boning up on IR best practices through NIRI classes and seminars to prepare for an IPO. I grew excited about the possibility of helping take the company public and ringing the bell on Wall Street.

One day running an errand at the nearby mall after work, I saw a missed call on my work cellphone. Back in those days, I carried two phones: my personal phone and my work phone, a Blackberry. One of our investors left a message. I listened to it and replayed it twice. He wanted to verify news about a strategic buyer acquiring Vangent

Say what? I hadn't heard anything from either Mac or Jim, so I called Jim and asked what this was all about. He asked me to disregard so I called the investor back and pretended I had no idea what he was talking about.

From that point on, the dominoes started falling quickly. Yes, indeed, the news was true. General Dynamics Information Technology, known as GDIT, made an offer Veritas Capital couldn't refuse. Vangent would be acquired by GDIT for $960 million, a hefty sum to pay for a company back then.

This was my first time going through a transaction like this. I had no idea what to expect. Phone calls and emails from reporters, investors, and employees came in from all directions. I prepared a holding statement that could neither confirm nor deny the transaction. As the details were still being hammered out, I merely acknowledged the development and said "no comment" to just about everyone.

I soon discovered my role and everyone else's on the executive team would vanish. It was a bit of a shock and happened quicker than I imagined.

It was the morning after Vangent won Government Contractor of the Year at the 9th Annual Greater Washington Government Contractor Awards Gala at the Ritz Carlton in Tysons Corner, Virginia. Champagne flowing and high fives galore commending me for a job well-done to secure the coveted industry award, I found out my job was eliminated. I was being "severed." While I scoped out opportunities at GDIT, a massive company with 100,000 employees globally, I never got an offer. And it wasn't for the lack of trying and networking with GDIT executives across the company, including its global operations.

I had to vacate my office in a few hours. Hours, not days. Just like that. Done. Over. Poof. Adios.

With tears in my eyes, I called Andy. In his usual comforting and understanding way, he helped me try to process what had just happened. "Babe, hang in there," he said. "You'll be fine. We'll be fine. I'll be there in a few hours. I love you."

As I sat in my office, staring out the window at a familiar vista overlooking the high rises in Ballston I had gotten to know over the years, I gazed around at nearly seven years of files, folders, books, binders, framed articles, artwork, knick-knacks, and tchotchkes. I was numb. It felt surreal. Deciding what to throw out, what to save, and what to leave behind felt like what people must go through when served an eviction notice.

When Andy arrived, we took about six boxes of artifacts and memories to our cars. After grabbing a couple of drinks across the street, I followed him to our church, and we caught the tail end of the evening mass. It happened to be the day after All Saints Day. Sitting in the pew, I looked up at the altar and prayed. This isn't how I imagined closing this chapter. But somehow, I knew my family's love and support would get us to a better place.

CHAPTER 6

THE SECRETS OF BETTER BRANDING FOR GOVERNMENT CONTRACTORS

The next morning, I woke up with a bad hangover but ready to start my usual routine. I then realized: I was in no rush. I was unemployed. For close to seven years, I'd automatically set my alarm clock for 5 a.m. to work out, prepare breakfast, pack lunches, nudge the kids out of bed, get them dressed, feed and then drive them to school to turn around and race home to hop in the shower, get myself ready, and speed like a crazy woman into the office to make my 9 a.m. meetings. It was a punishing routine, but my body had become conditioned to this rinse-and-repeat, every damn day.

Suddenly, everything came to a grinding halt.

Andy and I had previously planned a week-long trip to Paris, France, without the kids, so the timing of being unemployed couldn't have been better. Instead of having to squeeze in packing, getting the kids situated, and planning our itinerary between my work schedule, family duties, and finding new luggage to replace our beaten-up Samsonites, I took my time to get ready, made a trip to the mall (in the middle of the day, what a concept!), and leisurely prepared for a trip we'd long been anticipating.

It wasn't my first trip to France. In fact, I lived with a family during the summer before my senior year of high school in Moulins, a small city in the middle of the country, as an exchange student. I traveled to Paris several times during the Clinton Administration when I co-led a delegation with First Lady Hillary Rodham Clinton and a group of women business and government leaders to Paris in 1997 with Betsy Myers, who led the White House Women's Office and is the sister of Dee Dee Myers, the first woman to serve as White House press secretary. It was the trip of a lifetime. I used to make routine trips to Paris when I briefly worked at the International Youth Foundation leading corporate relations and partnering with companies like Danone.

Over those next couple of blurry days before our Paris vacation, I got phone calls, texts, and emails from friends and former coworkers. They couldn't believe what had happened to me. "How could this happen?" "You didn't deserve this!" and "You worked way too hard" were some of their reactions.

As I was still processing the whole incident, their care and concern comforted me greatly. The relationships I formed with so many people being in the trenches over the years felt like I was being voted off the island. While Andy kept assuring me, I shouldn't take any of it personally, it hurt a lot. So much blood, sweat, and tears had gone into this job and company. It was a lot to deal with.

The news of my departure spread like wildfire throughout the community. Soon, I received calls from close colleagues, like JD Kathuria, founder and CEO of WashingtonExec, the GovCon networking organization, who offered to help. One of the best investments of my time over those years was getting to know JD and being involved in WashingtonExec which helped me build relationships across the industry. To this day, I tremendously value networking, building, and maintaining relationships. I agree with something JD often says: It's too late to build a relationship when you need one.

After our divine Paris trip, where we explored the beautiful Champagne region, visited some of our favorite Champagne makers, and celebrated Andy's birthday, I returned home refreshed and ready to start a new chapter. With a new attitude, I began to think about a different future and how I could apply everything I knew toward building my own brand and business. *Could I actually hang my own shingle*?

On the plane back from Paris, I started writing in a notebook I brought on my trip. I was overwhelmed with so many ideas I needed to get out so I could start organizing my thoughts. I kept thinking, *There's so much I've done, so much I've accomplished. I've so much to offer.* I stopped beating myself up for being laid off and for feeling like a loser.

Instead, I was getting excited about how I could start telling my story to help people, companies, and organizations. It was exhilarating.

I knew I'd soon receive offers and opportunities to consider, thanks to my strong relationships and network. But I was in no rush to jump to another company. For the first time as a working mom, I took a needed breather from the rat race, spent time with my family, and did the thinking, writing, and planning I had always dreamed about.

I got in front of my computer and continued that blog I had begun on the plane. The ideas flowed like water out of a faucet. Night after night, I stayed up writing until 3 and 4 a.m. It was cathartic to write about everything I had done and strategies I created to help Vangent develop a valuable brand so well that it made me lose my job. *Wait a minute, is that what really happened?*

Over the next couple of days, I shaped that blog into my first article: "The Five Secrets of Better Branding for Government Contractors."

"There's a good reason Vangent was named Government Contractor of the Year at the 9th Annual Greater Washington Contractor Award gala."

"Vangent delivered great results and had a strong brand."

"Vangent's growth and market strength were the result of great customer service but also a strong focus on brand value, both internally and externally."

"Without a strong brand, many government services providers look exactly alike. With a solid and recognizable brand, a government services provider can come to stand for something valuable and important for its employees, customers, investors, and the citizenry it serves."

"Here are the five rules of branding I practiced at Vangent, which are essential for any company looking to enter the government services market, expand their market, or to re-position for growth opportunities."

When I wrapped up the article and showed it to Andy, who's one of the best editors I know (next to Camille Tuutti, who edited this book!), I thought, *Wow, this turned out pretty good, and it wasn't that hard to write.* Now, I just needed a platform to share it. The reporters I had pitched over the years came to mind. Would any of them be interested in *my story*?

I asked Nick Wakeman, editor-in-chief of Washington Technology. Nick is a leading reporter in the GovCon industry and a well-known and respected writer. I worked with Nick over the years and forged a good relationship. He's a great guy, fair and honest, and isn't in the game of writing "gotcha" stories. He had published many positive stories about EDS and Vangent. In fact, Mac framed the story Nick wrote about GDIT's acquisition of Vangent on Aug. 11, 2011, and gifted it to thank me for my role in the historic transaction.

I shared with Nick my new status and told him about my article. Without hesitation, he graciously offered to publish it. I was floored. I couldn't imagine a better platform to share my story. On Dec. 1, 2011, Washington Technology published "Five Secrets of Better Branding for Government Contractors." Nick wrote the subhead: "Branding can help deliver better results to enthuse employees and earn customer loyalty. Here's how."

Much to my surprise, my article started to gain attention. Companies reached out and asked me to become their brand consultant. A George Mason University business professor contacted me and asked if he could use my article in his course curriculum. Mark Amtower, the well-known author, speaker, and radio host, called and asked if he could interview me on Federal News Network about my article. It was a thrill to be on the air and share my story.

Following that interview, Nick told me my article was one of Washington Technology's top stories of 2011 — and when could I send him more?

Penning that first article and getting such positive reactions was the shot in the arm I needed to regain my confidence and feel good about forging my new path. As I took consulting gigs with companies, including Booz Allen Hamilton, I wrote more articles. "Four Reasons You Should Care About Social Responsibility" focused on the importance of developing, defining, and implementing corporate social responsibility programs, the predecessor to today's Environmental, Social, and Corporate Governance framework.

As I found my voice, I cranked out more stories. Over the next year, I wrote eight more pieces for Washington Technology. They included topics such as digital marketing, diversity, and inclusion, how to make "big-name hires" pay off, the importance of culture, customer experience, and crisis communications.

Twelve years later, as I reflect on these five secrets of better branding that caught the attention of Mark Amtower, who mentored me to write this book, I've applied these same golden rules to my roles leading communications, branding, and marketing at other top government contractors including Harris Corporation (now L3Harris), Cerner (now Oracle Health) and at Maximus today.

Focus on outcomes, not offerings. You can put a marketing brochure or a website of Company A next to Company B and cover up the names, and many people can't tell the difference. Why is that? Many companies list every offering in a "laundry list" fashion without explaining what problem or challenge they help their customers overcome. A much more compelling way to communicate what a company does differently is to promote the outcomes or results it accomplishes for its customers — in plain English.

At Vangent, I created an award-winning branding campaign on the fact that "four out of 10 Americans connect with Vangent, but never know it." We combined this powerful and memorable factoid with a unique result the company helped customers accomplish. Another example is the advertising campaign and thought leadership program I helped develop at Cerner. It was the first of its kind in the federal market. A webinar series called *Federal Pulse* showcased the company's insights on the importance of its role in implementing a new interoperable electronic health record system at the Department of Veterans Affairs and the Military Health System at the Defense Department.

Equip your employees with tools to be effective brand communicators. In the GovCon world, employees are your most valuable brand ambassadors. But the reality is most who work for government services providers can barely recite their company's mission or vision statements — let alone their menu of service offerings. The reason is simple: Mission statements often are too long and full of overused industry jargon.

Make it easy for your employees by giving them the tools to memorize the meaning or essence of your company's brand and internalize it so they can effectively explain what your company's brand means and represents. A brand playbook is useful to enlighten employees on the importance of what the brand means and how to explain it over the dinner table with their family.

Use easy words to describe your brand and "proof points" to help them convey what the brand represents. Brand playbooks can become an essential part of a company's onboarding program and can be reinforced with short, impactful videos.

Evoke emotions about your brand. It's OK, really! Companies marketing consumer products we buy and use daily are masters at making an emotional connection. They want you to feel good about buying and using their product. That's why today's consumer marketing focuses on how you feel versus how much the product costs or whether you need it. Why can't we apply that same rule to the government services market? You can.

Showcase your company's experts and thought leaders in conversations about pressing challenges facing its customers. What's the point in keeping their faces and insights behind nondescript bios or ho-hum descriptions of your company's services? Bring your company to life and use storytelling to create an emotional connection with your target audiences. Highlight your company's talent in rich content, quality authentic photos, and compelling videos. You'll offer your customers, teaming partners, and new recruits a glimpse into your company before they even meet you in person.

Your brand is your culture, and culture trumps strategy any day. The first question any new employee asks is about the company's culture, not its strategy. They want to know what it's like to work there, the environment, and the opportunities to advance their careers.

Many companies in the government services industry struggle to communicate their company culture. Instead, they give employees lists of customers, names of contract vehicles, and company locations. Does that answer an employee's questions about the company culture? Hardly.

Focus on core values and help employees understand how they do meaningful work and their impact on millions of people's lives every day. Permeate core values through employee and external communications in media relations, IR, marketing, and recruiting campaigns.

Invest in your company's brand, and don't be ashamed about it. "Don't be penny wise and pound foolish" rings true today in the government services industry, where pressure on top- and bottom-line growth has squeezed marketing, communications, advertising, and branding budgets.

In an era of competing resources in the federal government where blatant promotion is frowned upon, how do you distinguish your company and justify precious resources?

In a challenging economy like today's, upping your game and using inexpensive ways to showcase your company is crucial. Over the years, I've implemented integrated marketing programs with compelling and useful content utilizing social media tools, including Twitter, YouTube, LinkedIn, and Applecart, to drive brands directly to the audiences we need to reach. Yes, employees, customers, and investors do notice which companies have got it going on and which are stuck in the past.

CHAPTER 7

YOUR CULTURE IS YOUR BRAND

During the last 22 years working at GovCon and health technology companies, the concept of "culture" has come up quite a bit. The task of defining a corporate culture, getting buy-in and support, and making it come to life has been an interesting journey, to say the least.

While at EDS, I talked with folks across the business about Ross Perot and how his personality impacted the EDS culture. As Vangent was becoming a stand-alone, we discussed what part of the Pearson culture to keep and what to create anew.

I remember the rolling eyes when the subject of "corporate culture" came up with executive leadership. "Tell me something that'll help the company win more business, not cost money" was often a typical response. While the pushback didn't intimidate me, I knew they didn't understand the relationship between brand and culture. It was up to me to help them realize how a solid, differentiated company culture contributes to a strong, memorable, and effective brand.

Ultimately, I needed to help leadership see what actions to get the results everyone was looking for: a robust, healthy organization that operates with integrity and authenticity, and wins the competitive battle for customers and employees. Partnering with HR became a powerful alliance in the quest to define and build company culture.

"Corporate culture…[is] the only truly sustainable competitive advantage… Given enough time and money, your competitors can duplicate almost everything you've got working for you," wrote George Bradt, a bestselling author, a leading voice on leadership and onboarding strategy, and a senior contributor to Forbes. "They can hire away some of your best people. They can reverse engineer your processes. The only thing they can't duplicate is your culture."

As Bradt reminds us: "[a]ll music is made from the same 12 notes. All culture is made from the same five components: behaviors, relationships, attitudes, values, and environment… It's the way those notes or components are put together that makes things sing."

Any HR, marketing, or communications executive agrees: Cultivating, capturing, and communicating a corporate culture is one of her or his most challenging assignments, and sometimes harder than carrying a tune. And any HR, marketing, or communications professional can tell you corporate culture is one of the hardest subjects to raise and discuss with a CEO and leadership team.

A book I read about 10 years ago by James Greco, "Fostering a High-Performance Corporate Culture: Leading CEOs on Establishing Unified Goals and Driving Company-wide Accountability," helped me understand how to better engage executive leadership to enlist their support with corporate culture. The author shares stories about some of the world's best-recognized brands. One that stood out was about the former CEO of Bruegger's whose brands include Bruegger's Bagels and the French bistro La Madeleine.

Greco writes, "In a thriving company — and at Bruegger's — the culture not only echoes the mission, but the culture also executes the mission. An aligned culture allows a company to deliver because employees not only understand the what — how to make bagels, prepare meals, etc. — they also believe in the why — our goal to make each guest's day a little bit better."

Greco continues, "Once the 'what' and the 'why' are established, it is the CEO's responsibility to determine the 'who'…CEOs must communicate the mission and culture throughout the organization."

When I read this book, I thought: *How can I apply the success of one of the world's leading bagel companies to a GovCon business? And how could I get the attention of CEOs to help them understand their incredibly important role in developing the who, what, and why of corporate culture and the inextricable link between culture and business success?*

Denise Lee Yohn's article, "Why Your Company Culture Should Match Your Brand," talks about the benefits of a "single, unifying drive behind both your culture and your brand…you reap the benefits of a focused and aligned workforce. No one needs to expend extra energy figuring out what to do or how to act in order to achieve what you want your company to stand for in the world."

In my post-Vangent years, when consulting for companies and government contractors, I never pretended building and communicating a company culture was easy. In fact, I'd tell clients it was the opposite. I vividly remember a conversation with the late Gio Patterson, who led business development for SRA International before joining Vangent. Known as one of the best BD executives in the industry, Gio was passionate about building culture. She knew it was a strategic advantage to hire good people and win business. "Culture eats strategy for lunch," she used to tell me. I remember the first time I heard that from Gio. She explained that Peter Drucker, one of the best known and influential thinkers on management, came up with a similar expression — that culture eats strategy for breakfast — but that lunch is one of those meals we typically eat when we're at work or at the office!

She told me about the strong culture at SRA International led by Dr. Renato "Renny" DiPentima, renowned for his leadership and bringing people together to feel passionate about their work. Gio taught me a lot about the importance of talking openly and honestly about culture and how to get executive leadership on board to "own culture."

Through many conversations over lunch, Gio got me thinking differently about serving as a bridge to work with business leaders to get the culture everyone wants: a healthy work environment with inspired people who drive boundless growth. She kept reminding me that with persistence and tenacity, companies like Vangent eventually reap the rewards of building and breeding a solid, sustainable, and recognizable corporate culture.

Over the years, I consulted for startups and government contractors to help them build communications and marketing strategies to grow their brands and business. I kept hearing the same questions: *Can you help describe our culture? Then, can you help us communicate what our culture and brand mean? How long will it take? And how much will it cost?*

I narrowed my approach to three key essential approaches any government contractor, small or big, can use to build a winning corporate culture.

Translate your company's mission and vision into the why, what, and who (in plain English). Create easy-to-remember and easy-to-practice core values. Put it all together: mission, vision, values. We've all seen corporate mission statements not one employee knows or could recite, even if their life depended on it. Government contractors' mission statements are often laden with industry jargon and poorly constructed phraseology an average employee barely understands or relates to.

It's essential to clarify what your company does, why your company matters, and who's impacted by your company's good work. For the C-suite consumed with financial, legal, business development, and operations of the business, the why, what, and who aren't as evident.

While Bruegger's example of making its customer's day a little bit better may not intuitively translate to a GovCon business, it's actually not that far off! Think about something simple and perhaps altruistic every employee can grasp and get excited about.

Some of the best examples I've seen are from companies like Peraton, whose mission statement is a catchy, memorable phrase: *Do The Can't Be Done*. Another good example is Maximus, where I lead PR and communications: *Moving people forward*.

Ask your employees what they like about working at your company and what they hate — and don't forget to act on what your employees say needs fixing.

It's every dream of a CEO and chief human resources officer for their company to be known as a Great Place to Work, which has become corporate America's Good Housekeeping seal of approval.

Government contractors who go beyond the expected health insurance and 401K benefits by offering their employees a healthy working environment through shared ownership opportunities, or stock incentives, strong support for work/life/family balance, and creative professional and career development programs usually have low-employee turnover, high retention rates and ultimately, strong brand recognition.

Employee salaries and benefits represent the highest costs for today's government services providers. Instituting a regular feedback mechanism, such as employee satisfaction surveys, is one of the smartest actions companies can take to understand employees' needs, and interests and build a strong corporate culture.

Fostering a culture of listening, acting on what needs improvement, and then celebrating the benefits of new policies and programs go a long way in building a great place to work and a more valuable brand.

For small or startup companies, build your corporate culture around your CEO's personality, but remember, he or she is human. Let's face it, your CEO probably didn't become the CEO without strong and perhaps distinctive behaviors and traits attractive to investors, a board of directors, and top-notch people recruited to launch and grow a company. Relationships, reputation, expertise, financial acumen, and presentation skills undoubtedly were among their assets and attributes.

Starting a business or taking over a business is still considered the American Dream, and that's why employees, customers, and the media all love a good "rags to riches" story. People look up to entrepreneurs, and many admire their drive and determination to build a business that makes money and creates jobs. That's why many small and startups not only build their business around a strong founder or leader; they build their brand around his or her unique attributes.

To this day, I run into people who introduce themselves by saying who they used to work for, like David Mastran, the founder of Maximus, or Bob LaRose, the late Agilex Technologies co-founder and CEO, whose legacies are strongly revered in the GovCon community.

However, CEOs and entrepreneurs are human beings. Like everyone, they have strengths and weaknesses. What's important to remember about successful CEOs and company founders is that along their journey, they found a way to prevent their failings from becoming failures. Their story becomes their personal brand, and their personal brands become their company's brand and, ultimately, the foundation of their company's culture.

How companies tell that story — balancing confidence and humility — is the mark of a successful culture and brand. The late Tony Hsieh, the celebrated Zappos founder who sold his company to Amazon in 2009, stated it well: "Our belief is that if you get the culture right, most of the other stuff — like great customer service, or building a great long-term brand, or passionate employees and customers — will happen naturally on its own. Your culture is your brand."

CHAPTER 8

THE DREADED BUDGET: HOW I FINALLY LEARNED TO GET THE RESOURCES I NEEDED

As a young girl, I remember watching my mom, Jacqueline "Jackie" Ethel (nee Schaefer) Cassidy, manage our family budget. A gifted natural organizer with German practical roots, she grew up in a large family in Milwaukee in the aftermath of the Great Depression. Mom often shared how her siblings took baths, one after the other, to conserve water. Resources like hot water weren't as plentiful in some parts of the country back in the 1940s and early '50s as they're today. She applied those survival skills to raise our family in the early '70s and '80s. She showed my brother, Brian, and me how to cut coupons. She often wrote our family expenses on the back of an envelope: mortgage, car payment, insurance, gas, and groceries were listed with numbers next to them.

I never knew my parents' take-home pay, and honestly had no idea how much things cost back then. I knew they somehow stretched every penny to make ends meet. Mom taught us saving was important. When I wanted to buy a new pair of jeans or shoes, she said, "Why don't you save your money from babysitting, or from your job at Fox's Delicatessen, or from your newspaper route." And that's what I did.

When the time came for college, and I decided to go to an out-of-state school, my parents were extremely supportive but drilled into me that we needed student loans and financial aid to make it happen. I remember Mom sitting down with me as we filled out financial aid forms. She walked me through the tuition and room and board costs. It was as plain as day: There was a gap, but we'd figure out a way to make it work.

I took those memories of watching Mom manage our family budget to my roles as a government official and a business executive to develop and manage multimillion-dollar programs and budgets. Going to business school to get my MBA, as well as working in banking after undergraduate school, helped me develop essential financial management skills. Still, it was invaluable to watch a strong woman like Mom manage and run our family household.

But nothing truly prepared me for those early years helming the MarCom departments of GovCon companies. When it was time to come up with a budget, it seemed like everything I learned had to be thrown into the wind. Nothing made sense. As soon as I'd grasp the costs for things like personnel, trade association dues, subscriptions, sponsorships, marketing collateral, and trade shows, I'd ask questions like, *How do these costs support our strategic plan and our business development pipeline?* There were no good answers.

It took me a while — and several roles — to truly comprehend how much the budgeting process at a GovCon company differs from anything else I had ever experienced. And it also took me some time to fully grasp what skills I needed to negotiate the budget to do my job.

The stars started to align when I took on the IR role at Vangent. It gave me a bird's eye view of the cost structure across the company and how other departments formed their budgets. I gleaned greater insights into the pipeline of new sales opportunities and saw how I could build a MarCom budget tied to helping realize leads and wins.

In 2013, when I joined Harris Corp. (now L3 Harris) to lead MarCom for its healthcare division, I took those insights with me to work with a brilliant healthcare visionary, Dr. Vishal Agrawal, whom I connected with through my dear friend, Jaime O'Keefe.

Before joining Harris, Vishal attended medical school at Yale University and spent 12 years at McKinsey & Co. as a partner. He served in McKinsey's North American Healthcare Systems & Services Practice, and the company's private equity and principal investors practice. He's super connected and has one of the strongest business acumen I've ever seen.

It was exciting to work with Vishal and market a federal and commercial health business into a formidable player in the booming health technology industry. I felt like I won the lottery working with Vishal, who taught me a lot about the business of healthcare. I had a front seat to learn from him and market new technologies to improve the physician experience and create interoperability through business intelligence solutions across the continuum of care.

At Harris, I used my experience leading marketing, communications, and IR to build a budget that would factor in everything I knew we needed to do — starting with the first and most important step: market research. I was determined to get smarter about defining the problems the company wanted to solve and how best to reach our target audiences. The hardest part of that aspect was working out whom to trust to do the market research and how much to spend. I thought, *As soon as I figure out this important step, everything will fall into place.*

It wasn't that easy. It was a daunting task to create a budget to execute a MarCom plan and realize ambitious sales goals. It involved more than good common sense: it required selling my strategy and getting people to agree to it. And that's when I figured out how to get the budget I needed — I had to get different people on the same page and champion *our* collective strategy.

Over the next few months, I led a series of meetings with market research, product development, business development, finance, and HR. You name it, I got almost every facet of the business involved in our plan. Working backward from the revenue and profit goals we were on the hook to achieve, I constructed a step-by-step strategy to mature and market our technology solutions, reach target audiences, and convince them they needed our products and solutions over the competition.

I even convinced "Mother Harris" we needed a whole different website to reach our sales goals. At the time, the company's healthcare segment was a relatively small part of the overall business. When people searched for Harris Healthcare Solutions on the internet, they first saw images of tanks, military aircraft, warfighters, and men and women in uniform — the primary audience of Harris Corp. For the healthcare business to successfully reach providers, doctors, and health professionals, we needed to look like we were a healthcare company. And that required its own budget.

Putting together requirements from various business owners to reach our financial goals entailed people agreeing to measurements and metrics, such as how to define a new business lead and how and when that lead could be converted into a sale. From there, I could do the math to determine how much marketing dollars we needed to invest to reach target buyers and convince them to buy our patient or provider portal, for example.

Next, getting leadership buy-in and agreement as to what constituted a decent ROI for the overall marketing budget ask wasn't as clear as I had hoped. I worked hard to maintain the goalposts around a defined strategy within a set geography and timeframe, and yet constantly struggled to stop the goalposts from being moved. I learned holding executives' feet to the fire was critical to negotiate and agreeing to a marketing budget.

Harris' health technology business spent a significant amount of money from its marketing budget to take part in the yearly HIMSS conference. HIMSS stands for Healthcare Information Management Systems and Society and is one of the oldest and best-known non-profits in the healthcare technology space. It puts on one of the largest healthcare technology events that attract thousands of companies and tens of thousands of people who flock to places like Orlando, New Orleans, Las Vegas, or Chicago for four days of positioning, networking, and schmoozing. In my next chapter, *Why I Hate Trade Shows (and How To Survive Them)*, you'll read more about my feelings about trade shows.

Anyone who has ever planned to participate in the HIMSS conference knows how difficult it's to plan this event "on the cheap." Exhibiting at HIMSS pretty much gobbles up an entire budget. The real trick is laying out the costs and explaining there's truly an unknown ROI for participating in an event like that. Pretending there's a black-and-white or magical result, such as the number of people who watched a demo or picked up a tchotchke as a measurement of ROI, is ridiculous.

I eventually learned to budget for trade shows, including HIMSS, starting with what you think it'll cost — then multiply that by three. Don't ever fool yourself — or your executives — into thinking that participating and exhibiting at HIMSS — or similar high-cost trade shows — magically delivers leads to meeting or exceeding your sales targets. It's more about helping your executives understand the intrinsic value of being present, broadening your brand, deepening awareness, and establishing connections.

This brings me to my final point about compiling the dreaded budget. More than likely, those of you reading this book have submitted, fought for, and/or defended budget requests to support your company's MarCom activities — and have the battle scars and stories to prove it!

Throughout your budget planning process, you've likely eyed opportunities and new ways to deepen your company's brand visibility, jump-start a lead-generation campaign, upgrade your company's digital presence, diversify your company's participation in events, or create a totally new outreach strategy through social media. You may be in an even bolder place with a greater headcount to augment your already-overstretched staff to more effectively support your company's efforts to win new business and grow revenue.

Depending on your company's appetite for investing in branding and digital marketing, your role as a MarCom executive will differ in range, scope, and influence. No matter what, the MarCom budget will undoubtedly be scrutinized by executive management, who'll decide if doing the "same old, same old" with the current level of resources suffices. Or you might convince leadership how an infusion of new marketing dollars could boost revenues and give your company a leg up over the competition to differentiate your company's solutions, expertise, and results.

There are many schools of thought on this important question. While not black and white, the best way to argue for an additional budget is to tie marketing investment to realizing your company's strategic plan, business development goals, and, ultimately, stock price if your company is publicly traded.

I can't overemphasize the importance of regularly measuring and reporting the results and impact of your company's investment in MarCom activities. *That is when I figured out how to get the budget, I needed to do my job.* When developing that dreaded budget, you can use those reports to remind them what your current investment got them. If they want more, help them realize what it'll cost and what they should expect. That's your job as a marketing leader.

CHAPTER 9

WHY I HATE TRADE SHOWS (AND HOW TO SURVIVE THEM)

In my last chapter, I shared Mom's financial planning influence that helped me learn how to get the budget I needed to lead MarCom departments. In this chapter, I share my dad's influence with trade shows and how I grew to despise them but eventually learned to survive them.

Dad, the late Robert "Bob" Cassidy, who, like Mom, grew up in the aftermath of the Great Depression, was a gifted painter who made a living designing exhibits for museums. Growing up in Milwaukee, Wisconsin, and Rochester, New York, I went to exhibit openings at the museums where Dad worked. He was incredibly talented at building beautiful multi-dimensional exhibits that showcased an interesting time in history, a collection of anthropological discoveries, a selection of unique art objects, or stories about influential local leaders. He was an incredible storyteller but also had a knack for laying everything out in an aesthetically pleasing way. He artistically captured the colors, textures, and shapes down to the smallest details in those little signs that beautifully described the contents and stories behind the exhibits.

Sometimes, it took Dad and his team months — sometimes years — to finish an exhibit. Once it opened, the first night drew lines of people, news reporters and local leaders, who spent hours admiring Dad's unique designs and striking content. I'd watch Dad take VIPs around his exhibits, giving them an insider view into his magical touch. I was so proud to be his daughter.

Understandably, the bar for what constituted a stellar exhibit was raised high for me at a very early age, thanks in large part to Dad's influence and passion for design excellence.

Imagine how shocked I was when I began to participate in and lead trade shows in the GovCon industry. I couldn't believe what I saw.

In Chapter 2, I shared my observations from COMDEX, which was my first trade show. When I walked into the cavernous ballroom of the MGM Grand in Las Vegas in late 2001, two months after 9/11, everywhere I looked, there were gigantic edifices, twirling signs, and flashing monitors. People were pacing frenetically. Booth babes in high heels giving out European chocolates on doily-lined silver platters. The sensory overload was overwhelming. While I didn't have a role at that time leading trade shows, I thought: *When I have that responsibility one day, I'm sure as heck going to think hard about investing in trade shows and make sure they look better than these clunky, ugly monstrosities!*

When I joined Harris (the healthcare business was sold to NantHealth in 2015) and subsequent roles at Ciox and Talix, two health technology companies where I worked in 2016-19, as well as Cerner (now Oracle Health), building booths and developing strategies for trade shows became part of my repertoire leading MarCom

In all these companies, trade shows were thought of as a "necessary evil," as one sales leader put it.

"Say what?" was my reaction. "Where did you get that belief that it's a necessary evil?"

"We've got to be there. A good place on the floor. A nice booth. We must have cool giveaways. We need to throw a party."

"Why?" I asked.

"All our competitors are there and do it, so we have to be there, too," said my colleague.

"That is not a good answer. So, we're spending how much money to try to get the attention of our competitors, and for what purpose?" I pressed.

"Oh, no, our customers will be there. And our top prospects will come. We need to impress them," said a BD guy.

"So, a trade show where we're competing for eyeballs and attention with everyone else, that's going to help us make our growth and sales goals?" I asked.

"Oh, Eileen, we must be there. It's about brand awareness. And leads! Don't you get it? I know you'll figure it out."

Over the years, I heard that refrain over and over again. I challenged BD leaders I worked with — the biggest proponents of trade shows — to dig into why they were necessary and what we'd gain from attending. I pressed them to explain the ROI and why standing around a gigantic convention hall, trying to lure people into our booth and look at our latest application or solution, was the best use of our limited budget, time, and resources.

In my previous chapter, I talked about putting together a budget for the annual HIMSS show, the largest trade show I ever managed. If you've been to a HIMSS show, even in the post-COVID world, you might have thought companies have endless piles of money. For some companies, that may be true. But for the companies I worked with, I had to budget everything and fight for every penny. Everything has a cost, from the actual booth structure to the furniture you put in the booth, the monitors, and the videos you produce to show on those monitors.

What many don't realize is you need to pay to rent the space on the floor — which you typically reserve a year in advance. You also need to pay for electrical and internet service, transportation of the exhibit from the storage space to the floor, rigging signs, lighting exhibits, hooking up monitors, waste baskets, and vacuuming. The cappuccino machines and the people you hire to make and serve coffee in your booth. You name it. Everything has a line-item cost.

I'll never forget the February 2014 HIMSS show in Orlando, Florida. It was a month before I was scheduled for my second hip replacement. Yes, my second hip replacement! I had my right hip replaced in May 2008 after years of agonizing pain from premature osteoarthritis because of a car accident when I was 17. After almost six years of favoring my right hip, it finally gave up. I scheduled my hip replacement surgery right after the HIMSS show and after Andy, Carmen, and I took a much-anticipated trip to Disneyworld in Orlando.

As I was hobbling around the exhibit floor of the gigantic Orange County Convention Center, trying to get everything ready for the HIMSS show in a few hours, I was in major pain. Somehow, I kept it together, thanks to a great group of colleagues and a few bottles of Aleve. We decided at the last minute to kick in an extra thousand bucks to hang a Harris sign over our booth. While I wasn't convinced it was worth it, my BD colleagues complained it would be hard to find our booth if we didn't have a hanging sign. I told them I'd rather spend that money doing outbound direct marketing to help our customers and prospects understand the value of our technology and solutions. And, I argued, I could measure the return on investment and capture leads. *How do you measure ROI from a hanging sign?*

Needless to say, I lost that battle. I had to find a way to convince the rigging contractor to put our sign up, as it was already booked and had no more bandwidth. When I told the conference services guy we had already paid for the rigging cost, he told me he didn't have the order, and we were out of luck. How could that be? Around 11 p.m. the night before the conference, I walked up to a guy rigging a sign next to our booth. I told him about our dilemma. I pulled $100 in cash from my wallet and pleaded with him to hang our sign. He must have felt sorry for me, so he agreed. "Meet me at 2 a.m., and I'll help you out," he said. And that's how that stupid sign got up.

I have many more similar stories, but the point is: In all the years I've managed MarCom for government contractors, I never could rationalize the cost of exhibiting in a trade show. And unfortunately, and I wish it weren't true, there's no magical or secret way to measure what you get from the eye-popping costs. Many times, I sat down with BD leaders and executives pressured to participate in a trade show or conference and did the math for them. I walked through the costs line by line and helped them see just how much money we'd spend at a trade show and shared examples of other marketing, sponsorship, thought leadership, or advertising activities that could yield better results.

I understand trade shows and conferences are ways to meet and engage people, which is important to building relationships, broadening networks, and extending your brand, especially in a post-COVID world. However, I've never been convinced of being part of the tired, stale, and predicable format of today's trade shows where people stand or sit behind tables, wait for people to pass by, lure them with a tchotchke, and try convincing them to spend a minute listening to a gimmicky sales pitch.

While I've been on my anti-trade show crusade for a while, I've also helped companies develop differentiated customer engagement strategies and sponsorships — where you're not competing with hundreds of other companies — that produce more measurable and more impactful outcomes such as new contacts, deeper relationships with existing customers, sales leads with new customers, and stronger brand sentiment.

However, I fully recognize — and accept — that trade shows will likely never go away as they are cottage industries themselves.

As a way to survive trade shows and conferences, I developed four outcomes helpful to get BD, senior management, and executives on board and achieve the results you want.

Identify a quantifiable number of quality new business leads to grow your pipeline. Counting new business leads isn't easy. It's challenging to gauge someone's genuine interest in purchasing your company's products or services when walking into your booth, stopping to watch a video, or grabbing a tchotchke or hospitality item. Invest in pre-conference outreach to target new business prospects who will attend the show and preschedule meetings at your booth or another meeting space. That way, you can plan ahead to schedule demos or invite selected members of your team to participate in a certain discussion. Investing in lead generation software and devices is a must — the trick is to ensure your booth staff diligently tracks and codes the conversations. Just think, one sale from a lead can justify the entire trade show investment.

Educate your audiences face-to-face (as opposed to online). Think of participating in a trade show as creating that once-a-year bricks-and-mortar storefront so your customers and prospects can experience what it feels like to do business with your company. Unlike traditional retail companies, most government contractors don't have a showroom or storefront where their customers can walk in, play with devices, watch demos, and talk to real people.

Exhibiting at a trade show is that rare opportunity for your company to educate people about what you do, how you achieve results for your customers, and, most importantly, why your company's products and services have value. How do you ensure an effective education strategy? For starters, make sure your staff is trained in the full range of your company's products and services and knows how to talk about them. Not everyone knows how to actually talk to people — really.

Think carefully about the people you staff your booth with. Track how many people request demos, how many demos you give, and how many people request follow-up meetings and conversations. Collecting or, better yet — scanning business cards — is good, but what's even better is measuring how many of the people you targeted in your pre-show outreach actually make it to your booth.

Aggressively seek media and analyst coverage. In the 24/7/365 always-on news cycle, it's critical to target the audiences you want to reach. The trick is identifying how your audiences obtain information and news. Work with a solid and reputable PR firm that knows your audiences, which publications, news sources, and organizations they follow, and most importantly, has good contacts and can get interviews with.

In preparation for the trade show, develop a wish list of editors, bloggers, and analysts you want to reach and schedule appointments and meetings. As you prepare your trade show strategy, factor in the news announcements, white papers, and reports you'll want to release before the show. Then, determine which reporters you want to break your story.

Social media is huge, and many trade shows have a "social media ambassador" program where social media influencers are credentialed to attend the conference and have the same access as news media and professional bloggers. To assess the effectiveness of your media strategy, measure how many meetings you've requested vs. how many you can schedule, the number of feature articles, mentions, and news hits you generated, and the number of follow-up interviews and future stories you can plant.

Wow them. Think of a trade show as a playground for enthusiasts of your industry. It's important to carefully think and plan ahead the kind of experience you want people to have in "your" playground. Do you want people to look around, be overwhelmed, and walk away? Or do you want a person (your future customers) to see something that's a bit different, grab their attention, and have a conversation? We all want folks to stick around and be engaged. We, marketers, know how much it takes to get people really engaged. It's one of the most underestimated outcomes of any marketing endeavor. It's much harder than anyone thinks. So go ahead, be bold, be creative, and be inventive. Your exhibit presence reflects your brand.

CHAPTER 10

WHY MARCOM LEADERS NEED TO UNDERSTAND FEDERAL ACQUISITION REGULATIONS

I thought long and hard about writing this chapter as I fully get it's a dry and boring topic. However, I decided it was important for one major reason: It was a game-changer when I finally understood GovCon rules and regulations. And once I did, that knowledge made me a more valuable business leader.

As I shared, I led a relatively narrow "swim lane" when I first started in the GovCon industry over 20 years ago, responsible for EDS' PR in the company's federal business. At the time, I hadn't yet heard of the FAR — Federal Acquisition Regulation — known as the GovCon "bible." The FAR is "the primary regulation for use by all executive agencies in their acquisition of supplies and services with appropriated funds," as defined by the General Services Administration.

In subsequent companies where I was responsible for the full gamut of PR, marketing, communications, and IR activities, I got more familiar with the significance of the FAR and its impact on the MarCom role. It became my secret edge.

During those years, as I developed MarCom strategies, plans, and budgets, I started to hear terms like "allowable" and "unallowable" costs. I'd shake my head and wonder, *What the heck does that mean?*

What I grew to learn, the FAR spells out in black and white the "allowable" costs a government contractor can bill to its customer through a government contract and "unallowable" costs that can't be billed back. In other words, the FAR stipulates which costs a government contractor will get reimbursed for by its customer and which costs hit a company's bottom line and impact profitability.

At first, I didn't understand what this had to do with a MarCom leader. As I dug in and asked questions, I soon figured out why GovCon companies don't spend a lot of money on branding to blatantly call out favorable attention to their company. It's because they typically don't get reimbursed by their customers for the cost of advertising and PR activities, with a few exceptions. In addition, the FAR frowns upon "calling favorable attention to the contractor for purposes of enhancing the company image to sell the company's products or services."

According to the FAR, the term "public relations" means all the "functions and activities dedicated to maintaining, protecting, and enhancing the image of a concern or its products; or maintaining or promoting reciprocal understanding and favorable relations with the public at large, or any segment of the public." The FAR further clarifies PR "includes activities associated with such areas such as advertising and customer relations."

The FAR defines advertising as "the use of media to promote the sale of products or services and to accomplish the activities referred to in paragraph (d) of this subsection, regardless of the medium employed, when the advertiser has control over the form and content of what will appear, the media in which it will it appear, and when it will appear. Advertising media include but are not limited to conventions, exhibits, free goods, samples, magazines, trade papers, direct mail, dealer cards, window displays, outdoor advertising, radio, and television."

The FAR goes on to define the combination of PR and advertising costs to "include the costs of media time and space, purchased services performed by outside organizations, as well as the applicable portion of salaries, travel, and fringe benefits of employees engaged in the functions and activities identified in paragraphs (a) and (b) of this subsection."

For anyone who has studied and/or led PR and advertising, do these descriptions and definitions make intuitive sense? To me and most people I've met, they don't. What's also incredible about these definitions is the term "marketing" is totally absent. Kind of strange, right?

If you're still confused, you're not alone. What matters the most is to understand what costs are "allowable" and "unallowable." So, here are the only allowable advertising costs:

- Specifically required by the contract, or that arise from requirements of Government contracts, and that are exclusively for:
  - o Acquiring scarce items for contract performance, or
  - o Disposing of scrap or surplus materials acquired for contract performance

For many government contractors, especially those which perform technology, IT, and other types of related professional services, it's hard to imagine how any type of advertising is allowable.

There's a subsequent paragraph that describes "costs of activities to promote sales of products normally sold to the U.S. Government, including trade shows, which contain a significant effort to promote exports from the United States. Such costs are allowable, notwithstanding." That paragraph cites a bunch of unallowable PR and advertising costs, as well as other unallowable costs, including "memorabilia, alcoholic beverages, entertainment and physical facilities that are used primarily for entertainment rather than product promotion."

Other allowable public relations costs include:

- Costs specifically required by the contract
- Costs of responding to inquiries on company policies and activities, communicating with the public, press, stockholders, creditors, and customers
- Conducting general liaison with news media and Government public relations officers, to the extent that such activities are limited to communication and liaison necessary to keep the public informed on matters of public concern such as contract awards, plant closings or openings, employee layoffs or rehires, financial information, etc.
- Costs of participation in community service activities, such as blood bank drives, charity drives, savings bond drives, disaster assistance, etc.
- Costs of plant tours and open houses
- Costs of keel laying, ship laundering, commissioning, and roll-out ceremonies, to the extent specifically provided by the contract.

Unallowable public relations and advertising costs include:

- All public relations and advertising costs, other than those specified, whose primary purpose is to promote the sale of products or services by stimulating interest in a product or product line or by disseminating messages calling favorable attention to the contractor for purposes of enhancing the company image to sell the company's products or services.
- All costs of trade shows and other special events which do not contain a significant effort to promote the export sales of products normally sold to the U.S. Government
- Costs of sponsoring meetings, conventions, symposia, seminars, and other special events when the principal purpose of the event is other than dissemination of technical information or stimulation of production.
- Costs of ceremonies such as corporate celebrations and new product announcements
- Costs of promotional material, motion pictures, videotapes, brochures, handouts, magazines, and other media that are designed to call favorable attention to the contractor and its activities
- Costs of souvenirs, models, imprinted clothing, buttons, and other mementos provided to customers or the public
- Costs of memberships in civic and community organizations
- Costs associated with the donation of excess food to nonprofit organizations in accordance with the Federal Food Donation Act of 2008.

There's a lot to digest and understand with the FAR when applying these regulations to make sound business decisions. What makes it more challenging is many of the terms and descriptions appear outdated and out of touch with today's modern PR and advertising practices. It's hard to believe the FAR was updated in October 2022.

What are the takeaways for today's MarCom leaders? For sure, PR activities have the broadest leeway for being considered allowable costs. This is important to keep in mind as you guide your company in developing PR and media relations policies, processes, and guidelines. In addition, participation in community and philanthropic activities and events deserves attention, as well as how you allocate the budget and determine costs for trade shows.

I've summarized a few of my top considerations to understand how to interpret the FAR's acquisition regulations and apply that knowledge to plan and execute MarCom strategies:

Get to know your compliance and contracting officers. Ask them to explain how your company bills back any allowable costs for advertising and PR for your major contracts.

Once you have that information, analyze the costs your company incurs to perform marketing, advertising, and PR. Then, help your leadership understand what portion of your budget is considered allowable versus unallowable.

Break down your overall marketing budget into the FAR-defined categories of PR and advertising. Even though you may not necessarily manage or execute strategies along those lines, it's helpful for your leaders and teams to see, manage, and plan for these categories. Manage your unallowable marketing, PR, and advertising costs as frugally as possible.

Develop metrics to measure ROI to see which actions are effective in achieving your company's marketing and PR objectives. Whether increasing new business leads, expanding the share of the voice in the news media, improving brand and reputation sentiment, or dominating thought leadership for a critical growth area, every activity should be measured and evaluated.

I point this out for those in MarCom roles who haven't yet had someone sit down and explain the important nuances. To achieve tasks such as developing communication strategies, participating in trade shows, building contacts, or launching marketing campaigns, it's important to know which costs can be charged to government contracts. And it's equally vital to know which costs can't be reimbursed and, therefore, be considered strategic investments to achieve your company's business goals.

Ultimately, it's up to MarCom leaders to help executives understand the innate differences between marketing, PR, and advertising and why most companies, especially government contractors, need all three functions to work together to be successful.

CHAPTER 11

HOW TO EARN A SEAT AT THE TABLE — IT TAKES DETERMINATION, PERSEVERANCE, AND GROWING A PAIR OF COJONES

Looking back at my 22 years in GovCon, I recall realizing the value of having my voice finally heard. I want to share why it's critical for MarCom leaders to be present and accounted for.

First, I hearken back to my years working in the U.S. federal government. During the 1990s, when I served in the Clinton administration, I held several positions with varying degrees of responsibility and authority. In my first role at the Commerce Department, I was special assistant to Lauri J. Fitz-Pegado, director general and assistant secretary of the Commercial Service — *I know that's a mouthful.* As her special assistant, I was with her in just about every meeting to take notes, capture follow-up actions, and ensure she had the necessary backup for presentations. Being a special assistant comes with typically being the most senior right-hand in a federal office or bureau, and it taught me a lot about the importance of presence, preparation, and participation.

Supporting a high-level Black female government official helped me understand the importance of not just being at the table but also being an active participant to follow through to make a meaningful impact. Meeting after meeting, it became apparent who showed up unprepared and who brought their talking points, data, and supporting materials. Preparation and effective presentations with substantive input were key to moving your ideas forward and, ultimately, gaining power.

As I accompanied Lauri on trips, conferences, and meetings, I observed other senior government officials around the table listen intently to her every word, take notes, and nod in agreement. When she spoke, I watched the body language around the room to see who was listening, who was on board, who was being swayed, and whom we needed to work on. Lending an extra pair of eyeballs was important to my job as her assistant. I remember thinking, *When I eventually earn a seat at the table, this is how I want to be prepped and staffed!*

In my later roles as an assistant administrator for international trade at the Small Business Administration and then as the head of public affairs and spokesperson at the Peace Corps, which were equivalent to assistant secretary-level positions, I used the experience I gained to project more confidence than I would have been able to otherwise.

During meetings and interactions with agency leadership and my team, I made the most of the opportunity to educate my colleagues, provide valuable insights, make progress on projects, and gain input and support from others to ensure my success. I also listened to views from other stakeholders to inform my thinking and expand my understanding of different topics.

During my government roles, I understood that sitting at the table was a privilege, not a right. I took this responsibility seriously and valued the opportunity to contribute to discussions, explore new perspectives, and make good decisions with my team. As there was always a multitude of events, issues, and crises going on at any given time, being at the table meant you needed to be alert, current, attentive, and sharp.

Flash forward to when I transitioned from government to GovCon, it was a whole new world and a whole new culture. Although my private sector roles had similar or higher levels of authority and responsibility compared to my previous government positions, I found I wasn't included in leadership meetings or other important discussions where I could contribute, be heard, and participate in the conversation. I also discovered from the GovCon companies where I've worked, the role of a MarCom leader wasn't necessarily considered the same caliber or level of other roles with a seat at the table, such as the head of HR, the chief information officer or business segment leaders.

When I first joined EDS, my manager one day popped her head into my office and asked for a summary of what I was working on. I told her I'd be happy to share an update and then I asked, what did she need it for? Her response was elusive and vague. Turns out, she was going to a meeting to present a summary of my activities. In other words, she was presenting what I was doing *on my behalf.*

It was difficult for me to accept someone else representing me in a meeting I was supposed to attend. I had previously held government roles and felt less important in the GovCon company. *What was I, chopped liver?*

During my time in government, requests from my supervisor for updates on my work were transparent and part of a regular process. It was clear to me that sharing updates on my activities and projects was an important part of the larger picture. There was no drama, and the process was straightforward.

I often wondered why the role of a communications leader in government — typically the assistant secretary or head of public affairs — is a prominent leadership position that often reports to the secretary or deputy secretary — akin to the role of a CEO. Yet, in GovCon, with similar duties and responsibilities, the role is in a sub-reporting relationship and often relegated to the "kiddie table."

The communications and marketing leader, who supports pretty much all major functional areas of a business — as does the chief financial officer, head of HR, chief legal officer, and head of government relations — hasn't traditionally been at the table or considered part of the C-suite.

Yet, in the past couple of years, I've started seeing a shift. MarCom is getting elevated to the C-suite as the need for more strategic messaging and storytelling has immensely grown with the rise of social media, branded content, and corporate activism.

A recent Axios story, "The C-suite Shift," highlighted a January 2021 Edelman report called "The Future of Corporate Communications" that found 43% of communications teams are now centralized under the CEO — "a pivot away from reporting to marketing, human resources or legal functions." J.C. Lapierre, chief strategy and communications officer at PricewaterhouseCoopers, stated, "I'm talking to more CEOs every day who recognize that one of the most critical skill sets they need sitting by their side are communicators — and I include marketers in that."

A newer trend is for the marketing function to report to the communications leader. Lapierre, who reports to the PwC CEO, explains how PwC has benefitted by combining MarCom because her team "owns every channel, so you actually cannot get anything out that isn't aligned to the strategic agenda."

The Edelman report discussed how other companies, including IBM, are taking a similar approach to bring MarCom under a chief communications officer. IBM's Jonathan Adadshek, who's dual-hatted as chief communications officer and senior vice president of MarCom, says, "This reorganization allows the two teams to deliberately work together in a more streamlined way."

So, why is marketing coming under communications and not the other way around? John Connors, CEO of the Boathouse Group, a strategic consulting agency whose clever tagline, "humbly cutting through the bullshit," said: "It has more to do with marketers' history of pushing expensive, shiny objects instead of long-lead strategic planning. Agency presentations were reserved for lunchtime, and so we were treated like creative jesters…Over time, I think too many marketing people gave up the strategic high ground."

On the growing trend to place marketing under communications, Connors said: "Together, the two departments can build messaging campaigns that reach broad audiences. It's not just about reaching consumers anymore. There must be several issue narratives that companies can use to differentiate themselves among employees, consumers, legislators, and the media."

PwC's Lapierre stated, "By aligning with communications, marketers are better equipped to protect and promote the company's brand, and CEOs recognize that if they can use storytellers as strategic assets, they can help shape a strategy that is quicker to execute and will accelerate ROI."

The Axios article also reported on Boathouse's 2022 performance study, a quantitative analysis of 150 CEOs from leading companies nationwide about the role of chief marketing officers. The study found "less than half of CEOs trust their CMOs and only 25% believe their CMOs have strong decision-making skills." The highest grades from CEOs about their CMOs are because they trust them; the lowest grades are because they believe they can't drive company growth. It's a fascinating study that says a lot about what CEOs from top companies really think about the role of a CMO.

Could this be why MarCom has been relegated to the kiddie table in many GovCon companies? As a woman, I've often wondered if it has anything to do with gender, as most GovCon companies are led and run by men. However, I've started to see many of my peers, including women, being promoted to the C-suite, and more women are hired into communications and marketing leadership roles.

At Maximus, I was recently named to the corporate management team. I'm grateful to CEO Bruce Caswell and David Casey for their support in bringing my voice to the table.

What can communicators and marketers do to edge themselves into the C-suite and earn a seat at the table? I've been blessed to know and learn from many outstanding communicators and marketers over the years. Here are some best practices:

Help your CEO and C-suite understand the impact and ROI of your role. As a communicator or marketer, it's important to explain to your company's leaders how your efforts make progress toward increasing brand awareness, generating positive media coverage, mitigating negative media attention, or supporting important business deals and growth. Use understandable and relatable metrics to regularly track, evaluate, and measure your activities. Be punctual in providing reports. Don't just email and expect them to read your report; meet with them and take the time to walk through your analysis and answer their questions. Empower them!

Help your CEO and C-suite see you as a business leader and problem solver, not just a marketing or communications person. It's easy to fall into the trap of only focusing on MarCom. In addition to marketing and advertising campaigns, which you're expected to lead, your CEO and leadership need your help to apply MarCom skills to solve business problems. Identify gaps in the business beyond MarCom and step up to execute creative solutions. Show them you understand your company's business and wow them with creative communications for all the audiences you touch. It's not a one size fits all.

Be bold, creative, and visionary. "Go big or go home," an expression said to have originated as a sales slogan in the 1990s, still rings true today. Executives look for visionary strategies to drive home your company's strategic plan, differentiate your brand, and realize business goals. While small-muscle movements may have cut it years ago, it's imperative today to cut through the noise with bold and creative approaches to develop and deepen brand awareness with customers, employees, and on Capitol Hill. Think big!

Help your leaders understand communications and marketing are really two different functions, but by effectively working together, they can directly impact growth. The Axios article talked about how "communicators and marketers are magnetic forces that can either attract or repel. Communicators must lead by crafting clear messaging that aligns with company strategy, and marketers should use those narratives to attract the widest audience." Show your CEO and leadership you really do two different things —- and you know the secret combination. The name of the game is growth.

Finally, grow a pair of cojones. If you don't know what it means, Google it.

CHAPTER 12

THE FUTURE: WHY GOVCON NEEDS POWERHOUSE MARCOM LEADERS NOW MORE THAN EVER

As I wrap up the final chapter, I feel equal parts joy, pride, amazement, and excitement. It's taken me a long time to get to this point!

Here, I share some of my most inner and deepest thoughts and observations as a woman who fell into MarCom in the GovCon industry – by accident. And I also share why I believe — now more than ever — the industry needs powerful, resilient, and skilled communicators and marketers to get inside companies, step up, show them how it's done and make a difference — and do the *hard talk*. There's plenty of opportunity, and I'm living proof of it.

As I shared, when I got into a MarCom role in the GovCon industry more than two decades ago, it was far from my first choice. Honestly, I was preparing for my post-government career to join a global corporation as general manager of a geographic region. The idea was to leverage the language skills, knowledge, relationships, and networks I built in politics and serving in a presidential administration and become a business executive.

I'll never forget an opportunity I explored with Diageo, the multinational alcoholic beverage company headquartered in London. Through a referral from my friend Maria Tildon, whom I worked with in the Clinton administration, I was approached by Diageo to run its Latin America business. With operations in 132 sites around the world, the company is best known for iconic brands such as Johnnie Walker, Crown Royal, Smirnoff, Captain Morgan, Tanqueray, and Guinness.

In late 2000, when I was wrapping up my tenure in the Clinton administration, and it wasn't looking too good for Al Gore to become the next president, I engaged with Diageo about joining the company. It seemed like a great fit — I'd run a major business segment and run its Latin America operations. The only hitch was I needed to move from my home in Alexandria, Virginia, to Miami, Florida. As I was going through a divorce and a custody battle with my ex-husband, my son, Kyle, was my top priority. Picking up and relocating to Miami wasn't in the cards.

It was during that time my eyes opened to the world of GovCon as the next stop in my career journey. While I had heard of companies around the Beltway like Northrop Grumman, Boeing, Lockheed Martin, and even EDS — where I eventually joined — I couldn't see myself working for a company so closely aligned with the defense industry. There's nothing wrong with the defense industry, and believe me, many people I know, admire, and respect have worked or served at DOD – including my husband, Andy — who went on to exciting and rewarding careers in the defense sector. But I couldn't see myself being part of the defense and military arsenal.

As a young, idealistic woman who studied international relations, considered serving in the Peace Corps, and pursued a career in development banking and PR before getting into politics, working for a defense contractor didn't feel right. I was more interested in applying my talent and passions to help people get ahead in their lives, whether through education, healthcare, or social services.

I think that passion came from having lived in Mexico City in the mid-1980s and visiting countries with extreme poverty and dire living conditions. Places like Soweto in South Africa, the favelas in Rio de Janeiro, Brazil, and the territories of Gaza and the West Bank in the Middle East are just a few examples. After leaving government service, I was moved to join a company helping the less fortunate with the basics.

While I was familiar with the defense industry, having worked at EDS, Vangent, and later Harris Corp., and understood defense and military agencies need contractors to support warfighters to fulfill our country's missions around the world, it wasn't where I wanted to make a difference. I gravitated toward government programs like Medicare, Medicaid, Federal Student Aid, and support for our nation's veterans, and that's where I decided to develop more knowledge and expertise.

I developed a moral compass to help me make career decisions. By the end of 2011, I started using that compass to decide where to work and whom to work with, and how to make a positive impact.

The power of saying "No, I'm not interested" and backing it up with *hard talk* about the "why" proved useful in helping me make important career decisions. It also helped me become better known and respected as a communications and marketing leader grounded in healthcare and education. That's also how I eventually carved out a niche for myself.

A fair amount of luck helped me meet people like Vishal Agrawal, with whom I had the fortune of working with over five years at Harris and Ciox. He gave me a master class in understanding the healthcare system from the perspective of a provider, a payer, and a technology provider. But I'm also convinced my moral compass played a key role.

That compass also led me to Brandon Fureigh, who hired me in 2019 at Cerner, now Oracle Health. He and I met shortly after Cerner won two major contracts with DOD and VA to modernize electronic health record systems for veterans and service members and create "a lifetime of seamless care." He told me Cerner needed help to build, shape, and lead its federal marketing, communications, and PR strategies during a critical time for the company's growth and history. It was a terrific opportunity to develop Cerner's federal marketing strategies, help put the company on the proverbial map, and create a buzz inside and outside the Beltway.

When Brandon and I first met at a coffee shop in Old Town Alexandria, he didn't know me from Adam. But he did know my reputation and background in government and politics — a shared interest for the two of us and knew I'd be a good fit for what Cerner needed to build its brand and awareness in the federal marketplace. I'm forever grateful for having worked with Brandon and the team he built at Cerner.

That same compass led me to Elizabeth Smith, whom I briefly worked with at EDS. Elizabeth is one of the smartest and most talented business leaders I've ever known. After our brief time working together, Elizabeth reached out 15 years later to join her at Optum Federal, where she led business development. Unfortunately, the opportunity wasn't the right fit. A few years later, she reached out again about an opportunity at Maximus to lead PR and external communications. She introduced me to David Casey, who heads government relations and has been with the company in a variety of positions for almost thirty years. Working together, we create relationships with and advise government officials who develop, implement, and oversee public policy. We also work closely with national and international organizations across the branches of government.

I could go on and on about how I continue to use that compass to this day to guide my career decisions.

Government contractors face myriad challenges, including finding ways to grow profitably, aligning investments around a strategic plan, building a better customer experience, creating an engagement plan to retain and attract talent, modernizing technology platforms, charting a new course to moving from reactive to proactive PR, broadening brand awareness to win business, or creating a better process for rapid response and crisis communications.

All that requires rockstar and powerhouse communications and marketing leaders to make it happen and an ability to use "hard talk" to have difficult yet essential conversations to make progress in ways your company's leadership may not have initially considered or felt comfortable pursuing. Holding their hand, walking them through the details, and explaining how a carefully orchestrated and coordinated strategy can produce results to position your company for growth beyond the immediate crises are essential skills for today's public relations, marketing, and communications leaders.

I posed a question to some colleagues about the qualities they believe MarCom leaders need to succeed.

"One of the most important traits I look for in employees and future-ready leaders is curiosity and learning agility. With the rate of change, marketing and communication teams need to pivot faster to respond to rapidly changing customer and business dynamics. Equally, alignment to a strong value system is fundamental, if there is accountability, trust, and transparency, leaders feel empowered, and teams perform with purpose," shared Oliver Nutt, vice president of marketing and external communications at General Dynamics Information Technology. Oliver and I worked together at Vangent, and over the past several years, we've collaborated on the WashingtonExec MarCom Council.

Carl Dickson, the founder of CapturePLANNING.com and PROPLibrary, whom I have gotten to know through Mark Amtower's esteemed mentee group, shared another perspective. "The ability to provide customers with new reasons why they should care about you and recognize that you are their best alternative is what will overcome the challenges of the future. While methods and tools will change, MarCom will be needed more than ever to provide companies with the empathy and an understanding of what matters."

Joyce Bosc, whom I've known for more than 15 years, is one of the best PR pros in the GovCon industry. In 1978, she founded Boscobel Communications as a certified woman-owned business and has been advising GovCon companies for more than four decades. She offered another important perspective. "Government is an industry deeply rooted in trust and service. People commit their careers to protecting our nation and to serving our citizens. Looking into the future, there are growing and pressing reasons for the government and industry to collaborate. Together, we need to adapt and harden our technology innovations coming from the commercial sector for defense purposes. At the same time, seasoned government professionals are retiring, leaving the work to less-experienced personnel who will continue to be eager for education and support."

Bosc added, "GovCon communicators have a unique and important role to play. We connect companies and leaders with the government, to deliver the education, support, and solutions that advance missions. It starts with education. Ours is a service-oriented, trust-driven market. And it's up to us to insist that our companies are educating the market with expert thought leadership, not selling their wares. Over time, trust will come. Then, and only then, will GovCons earn the opportunity to secure a contract award."

Jim Miller, a trusted advisor to Maximus CEO Bruce Caswell and David Casey, has helped me in immeasurable ways over the past two years. He offered another important viewpoint. "Today, the public's trust in government is at a low ebb. Hyper-partisanship, narrow legislative majorities, and eroding sentiments toward the judiciary coincide with structural shifts in the economy caused by a worldwide pandemic, the war in Ukraine, and the accelerating impacts of global climate change, which has created a set of market conditions unlike any of those seen in current lifetimes. Adding to these external challenges is the government's inability to maintain a workforce of career professionals and the erosion of institutional knowledge. For these reasons, the demands on and role of government contractors is changing, and with it the demands on government contracting MarCom leaders."

Miller summed up the essential characteristics, talents, and skill sets of a "powerhouse" MarCom leader:

- **Thinks relationally.** With so many different variables flying around, most of which are outside one's control, the ability to identify, consider and apply the right mix of marketing to the issues is essential.

- **Understands utility.** The standard B2C/B2B marketing metrics aren't a good fit in business-to-government marketing or B2G. A powerhouse B2G leader needs to understand how to develop metrics that measure and move the needle on public trust, the utility that matters in B2G.

- **Knows the information economy.** The government is transitioning toward being a part of the information economy. A powerhouse MarCom leader must know what works and doesn't, and have solid experience and skills to create value from within this realm.

- **Marginal value creation.** All decisions are made on the margin benefits at the decision point. A powerhouse MarCom leader knows how to create and show marginal value creation that sustains across the planning horizon.

- **Builds trust.** An information economy is built on trust through the elimination of asymmetric information dynamics. B2G buyers are working in the public trust. A powerhouse MarCom leader understands how to build and maintain trust.

As government and military leaders retire, segue from political appointments, or decide to move into the private sector, I urge them to consider GovCon companies as the next stop in their careers. Their experience, perspectives, and understanding of how government works is a huge asset to government services companies.

Kelly Ceballos, who recently joined Maximus as senior director of PR and is my right hand, was previously deputy director of media relations for the Centers for Medicare and Medicaid Services. She also spent several years leading PR at CareFirst BlueCross BlueShield. We worked together in the early years of the Clinton administration at the Commerce Department when she was deputy press secretary. Her knowledge and relationships are already making a big difference in helping Maximus support our CMS customer as well as other clients.

As younger generations go to college and get out into the workforce, trying to figure out where they can land a job and make a difference, I urge them to study communications, PR, public affairs, media relations, and marketing — even as a minor or another field of study. Whether they decide to pursue communications or marketing full-time, we need millennials to Generation X and Z —the leading edge of our country's changing racial and ethnic makeup — as digital natives, they can help government contractors better support their customers and the people and constituents they serve every day.

People just like us.

ABOUT THE AUTHOR

Eileen Cassidy Rivera is an award-winning corporate and government executive, public affairs strategist, and policy leader known for her ability to quickly analyze and process complex information, zero in on strategic solutions, and creatively communicate to engage and persuade target audiences.

Eileen is Vice President of Public Relations and External Communications at Maximus (NYSE: MMS), where she shapes and builds Maximus' awareness and reputation as a leading provider of government services to Federal, state, and global governments.

In 2020, 2022, and 2023, WashingtonExec named Eileen one of the top Marketing and Communications Leaders to Watch.

Before joining Maximus in 2021, Eileen held senior roles in communications and marketing at other leading government contracting and healthcare technology companies, including Cerner (now Oracle Health), Ciox, Harris Healthcare Solutions (now L3Harris), Vangent (now GDIT) and Electronic Data Systems (now HP Enterprise).

Prior to her successful corporate career, Eileen worked at the former National Bank of Washington and the renowned public affairs agency Hill

& Knowlton. In 1993, she joined the Clinton Administration, where she led international trade and export promotion programs at the Department of Commerce and the Small Business Administration. At Commerce, she served as Special Assistant to the Assistant Secretary and Director General of the U.S. and Foreign Commercial Service in the International Trade Administration.

Working closely with the late Commerce Secretary Ronald H. Brown, Eileen developed and implemented a marketing and branding strategy for the Commercial Service. She helped create the new logo, which is still used today, and promoted newly formed U.S. Export Assistance Centers across the country. She also served as Deputy Director of the Office of Business Liaison in the Office of the Secretary of Commerce, where she led trade missions to the Middle East, Latin America, and South Africa.

At the Small Business Administration, Eileen was Assistant Administrator and Director of International Trade, where she promoted finance programs and initiated partnerships with Ireland, Egypt, Mexico, and Russia. She led trade missions to Asia, Latin America, and Europe. Vice President Al Gore selected the Export Express program, created by Eileen, for the National Partnership for Reinventing Government Hammer Award.

In the final year of the Clinton Administration, Eileen served as Director of Press and Public Affairs at the Peace Corps.

Furthering the late Secretary of Commerce Ron Brown's dedication to public service, Eileen serves on the Advisory Board of the Ron Brown Scholar Program, which encourages civic engagement among young African Americans of outstanding promise while promoting academic excellence, community, and lifelong interactions through academic scholarships, service opportunities, and leadership experiences.

Eileen was named by former VA Governors Terry McAuliffe and Ralph Northam to the Board of Visitors of Gunston Hall, the home of George Mason, who wrote Virginia's first Constitution and the Virginia Declaration of Rights, the precursor to the U.S. Constitution.

In 2006, Eileen was elected to the School Board of Alexandria City Public Schools and served until 2009. At the end of her term, Eileen was named Education Advocate of the Year by Tenants and Workers United for her efforts to close the achievement gap for minority and disabled students.

A proud Alexandrian, Eileen served on the boards of Agenda Alexandria, Commission for Women for the City of Alexandria, and First Night Alexandria, the preeminent New Year's Eve celebration for the Washington D.C. metropolitan area. Eileen also served as a volunteer with the Alexandria Medical Reserve Corps.

Born in Milwaukee, Wisconsin and raised in Rochester New York, Eileen graduated from American University with a B.A. in international studies and a M.B.A. in international business. She also studied at the Universidad Nacional Autónoma de México in Mexico City, Mexico and the Kennedy School of Government.

Eileen's pride and joy are her children, Kyle and Carmen, and her stepson, Drew. She is married to Andrew A. Rivera, a lawyer and policy analyst at the U.S. Department of Defense.

ACKNOWLEDGMENTS

I've been fortunate to pursue my dreams, including motherhood, studying at American University, playing flag football in Mexico City, working for the Clinton administration, getting elected, serving my community, using my language skills, becoming an executive, and writing my first book.

None of this would have been possible without the unwavering support of my parents, Bob and Jackie, who raised me to be adventurous, driven, caring, and compassionate. I'm lucky to have spent many great years with Mom and Dad, as a kid growing up in Milwaukee and Rochester, to all the times they visited me in Mexico City, Washington, D.C., Baltimore, Maryland, Arlington, and Alexandria, Virginia over the past 26 years. I was happy when Mom and Dad decided to finally pull up their roots in Milwaukee and move to Annapolis in 2007. Being closer allowed us to spend more quality time together. It's been wonderful to see our kids develop a close relationship with their grandparents. It's been three years since Dad left us. I'll forever miss his warm hands, twinkling smile, and deep love. I'm lucky to still have Mom in my life. She's my source of energy, wisdom, and great recipes.

My life over the past 19-plus years has been incredibly enriched through the love and support of my husband, Andy. When we first met in 1996 as political appointees in the Clinton administration, we both wanted a life where we could support each other's goals, aspirations, and dreams, and create new memories together. We've been through a lot over these years. I couldn't imagine my life without my best friend, soul mate, and ride-or-die partner.

Our kids, Kyle, Drew, and Carmen are my rock. While it hasn't been easy for Kyle and Drew navigating two homes and two families, I hope the resilience and strength they developed will help them lead happy, fulfilling, and successful lives. I pray every day for Kyle, who struggles with depression. I truly hope he finds the light to help him see the beauty and possibilities of what I know he can become.

Carmen is my angel. She's lucky to have two older brothers who love and look after her. She'll always be my Carmencita.

My brother, Brian, is a combo of my BFF and confidante. We've been by each other's sides through thick and thin. I'm incredibly grateful for his love and support, no matter what, and for creating the best book website. His wife, Lauren, is an amazing human and such a talent. My brother was very lucky to have met her!

I also want to give a huge shout-out to my amazing extended family — there are so many on both sides— but I wouldn't be the person I'm today without the love and support from the Cassidy, Schaefer, Rivera, D'Amour, Abrams, Maulucci, and Chiariello peeps!

There are so many people I've been blessed to know and learn from over these past five decades. I'm going to start with Karen Baskin, who was our next-door neighbor when we moved to Rochester in 1973. She's the sister I never had. I'm grateful for her friendship, great advice, love, and compassion over the past 50 years. Karen and her wife, Kim Grennan, are our extended family I'll forever cherish.

I wouldn't be the person I'm today without knowing and learning from Sheila Myers. Many moons ago, we spent our weekends as two Catholic girls working at the renowned Jewish delicatessen in Rochester, NY, Fox's Deli. Who would have thought we could turn our passion for lox and bagels and scooping gefilte fish into writing books? Sheila is now an award-winning author and college professor who inspired me to write this book. I'm deeply grateful for our friendship and everything I've learned from her.

As I was wrapping up my final year of business school at American University, working during the day as an aspiring investment banker at the former National Bank of Washington (NBW), a life-changing conversation over a cup of coffee led me to discover a whole new world at Hill+Knowlton. I wish I could recall the name of that super nice woman I worked with at NBW who introduced me to her client from Hill+Knowlton. The internship that resulted from this connection had a profound impact on my life. If you're reading this book, I can't thank you enough! That introduction opened my eyes to a world I never imagined.

I've been fortunate to know and work with Jill Schuker and Lauri Fitz-Pegado. Jill hired me as an intern at Hill+Knowlton in my last semester of business school. When I graduated, Lauri hired me to work in H+K's international division. I'm grateful they believed in me when I didn't know what the heck I was doing. We all went on together to work in the Clinton administration for the late Ron Brown at the Commerce Department. They took me under their wings and taught me skills that benefited me in countless ways, everything from learning how to write, manage people, dress, hone my political instincts, and get stuff done. They were my first mentors who held my hand until I was ready to jump off the deep end. I wouldn't have been able to swim and explore other oceans without their wise counsel.

I also worked with and learned from other exceptional people at H+K, including the late Bob Gray, the late Frank Mankiewicz, the late Jim Jennings, the late Joseph "Jay" Watkins, the late Laurel Laidlaw, Bob Witeck, Jeff Trammell, Gary Hymel, Arzu Tuncata, Barbara Coons, David Pryor, David Leavy, Sally Aman, John Berard, Lisa Binzel, Ellen Lathem, Diane Cardwell, Erica Venzke Amestoy, Meg Bender, Phil Armstrong, and Frank Kauffman, and many others.

Experiencing the thrill of becoming a public affairs strategist wouldn't have been the same if I hadn't worked side by side with my buddy, Katie Moore. We went through a lot together over those years, slugging it out at H+K and the Commerce Department. I'm forever grateful for Katie's friendship and her endless source of funny jokes, particularly while we were trying to learn Portuguese.

Lauri introduced me to the late Ron Brown, and through that relationship is how I became a political appointee in the Clinton administration. Working with Ron and traveling with him across the U.S. and places including Brazil, Israel, the Gaza Strip, and the West Bank were major highlights of my life. I'll never forget my first trip with Secretary Brown to Seattle, Washington, where I led policy advance for the Asia Pacific Economic Cooperation (APEC) meeting. Policy advance is an activity related to preparing a principal, such as a cabinet secretary, for policy discussions and events. Representing Secretary Brown at that meeting was an honor of a lifetime.

The day Secretary Brown and 34 others, including good friends I met at the Commerce Department, died in a plane crash in Croatia was a life-changing moment for me. I lost many dear friends and colleagues, including Lawrence "Lawry" Payne, Gail Dobert, Kathryn Kellogg, William "Bill" Morton, Adam Darling, Carol Hamilton, Kathryn Hoffman, and Charles Meissner. These brave people were leading a trade mission of business executives to the former Yugoslavia to explore business opportunities to rebuild the war-torn region. The day they perished, April 3, 1996, is a date forever seared in my memory. I dedicate this book to Secretary Brown and the friends I lost and whom I miss to this day.

While at the Commerce Department, I worked alongside other exceptional people I was fortunate to learn from, including Jeff Garten, David Rothkopf, Bob LaRussa, Jim Hackney, Dan McLaughlin, Cecile Ablack, Shari Gersten, Maria Cardona, Anne Alonzo, Ted Carr, Sally Painter, Clyde Robinson, Sue Esserman, Rob Klein, Lisa Walker, Dao Le, Andrew Balfour, Carola McGiffert, Larry Irving, Rich Gannon, Jonathan Greenblatt, Rich Rodgers, Claudia Rayford Rodgers, Jose Ceballos, Kelly Leeds (now Ceballos), Bettie Baca, Alison Kutler, Julie Rice, Melissa Moss, Loretta Dunn (now Schmitzer), Sally Susman, Bill Buck, Norma Krayem, Michelle O'Neill, Dalia Elalfi Spicer, Barbara Fredericks, Barbara Schmitz, Mary Fran Kirchner, and many others. During those incredible years, I formed a special bond with a group of amazing women, including Pilar Martinez, Charlotte Kea, Maria Tildon and Marian Pegram, whom I keep in close touch with to this day. I'm grateful for everything I learned from my Commerce family.

When I transitioned to the SBA, I had the privilege of working with another group of exceptional people, including Phil Lader, Cassandra Pulley, Ginger Lew, Aida Alvarez, Fred Hochberg, Jorge Valencia, Ira Sockowitz,

Jenny Dominguez, Wendy Goldberg, Jamal Simmons, Jean Smith, Nancy Smith-Nissley, Richard Ginsberg, Sherrye Henry, Betsy Myers, Julie Palermo, among many others. I'm grateful for everything I learned from my SBA family.

Between SBA and the Peace Corps, I spent a year at the International Youth Foundation in Baltimore, where I led corporate relations and an end-of-millennium fundraising campaign called Children's Hour. I'm grateful to Aaron Williams for taking me under his wings. I learned a lot from working with Aaron. He's one of the kindest people and most talented leaders I've ever known, who went on to be the director of the Peace Corps during the Obama administration. I'm also grateful for working with and learning from Rick Little, Bill Reese, Dick Schubert, Julie Rice, and others. I appreciate everything I learned from my IYF family.

During my brief year at the Peace Corps, I was fortunate to work alongside some passionate and talented people, including Mark Schneider, Tom Tighe, and Mike Chapman. I'm forever grateful for the opportunity to be part of one of the most amazing U.S. government programs that train and deploy volunteers to provide international development assistance to people around the world.

The two-plus decades I've been in the GovCon and healthcare industries have had their share of ups and downs. I'm blessed to have gotten to know and work with people who've mentored me and shown me the ropes at companies including EDS (now HP Enterprise), Pearson Government Solutions (which became Vangent and sold to GDIT), Harris Healthcare Solutions (which was sold to NantHealth), Harris Corp. (which became L3Harris), Ciox, Talix, Cerner (which became Oracle Health) and Maximus. Many people I worked with had a profound influence on my career, including Laura Lewis (now Mead), Elizabeth Smith, Al Edmonds, Bill Ritz, Bill Sweeney, Anne Reed, Kay Goss, Bill McGovern, Adnan Malik, Mac Curtis, Jim Reagan, the late Gio Patterson, Trang Mar, Manny Mar, Jeanne O'Kelley, Pam Thompson Stewart, Erik Buice, Jeff Bohling, Jerry Calhoun, John George, Dave Fabianski, Dick Bottorff, Judy Martin, Jan Lamoglia, Jeri Kirschner, Scott Stewart, James. Gordon, Chad Thyes, Emily Markmann, Vishal Agrawal, Jaime Orlando, Melody Pleasure, Lorely Flores, Michelle Pinto Mege, Bob Hetchler, Brandon Fureigh, Josh Hillebrand, Mark Mellott, Sherry MacDonald, Jennifer Cassou, Travis Dalton, Joe Mandacina, Brian Sandager, Kip Payne, Peter Henry, Danielle Applegate, and many others. At Maximus, I am grateful for the support of colleagues I'm privileged to work with every day, including David Casey, who has been a wonderful mentor, and Bruce Caswell, president and CEO, who's a great leader. I value the partnerships with my colleagues including Kelly Ceballos, Ilene Baylinson, David Mutryn, Kevin Reilly, John Lambeth, Terry Weipert, Michelle Link, David Francis, Bruce Perkins, James Dunn, Lisa Simmons, Arvenita Washington Cherry, Keely Wilson, Jude Metoyer, Jim Miller, Pam Corbett, Jessica Batt, James Francis, Jared Curtis, Dianne Henderson, Liz Anthony, Heather Shingleton, T.J. Davis, Justin Wills, Chris Mirro, Juliane Swatt, Lou Shields, Dave Harkess, Julia Willis, and many others. I am also grateful for the opportunity to build relationships and gain insights with PR and public affairs agencies I've been lucky to work with, including Sean O'Leary and Susan Davis at Susan Davis International and Liz Halloran, Ben Sheidler, Matt Paul, and Paul DiNino at Cornerstone.

I'm also indebted to friendships with my close friends, many of whom I met while studying at American University, including Laura Lewis Mead, Chris Mead, Marie (Demer) Rader, Amy and David Boris, Katie and Greg

Martinez, Kumar Belle, Eugene and Laura Smith, Sunil and Sarah Shamlal, Zoanne Nelson, Al Chan, and Geralynn Francheschini.

While studying at American as an undergraduate, I met some fantastic people who remain close friends to this day, including Antonio "Tony" Izzo and Allison Silberberg. Tony and I had some great adventures together in Florida and the U.K. that I'll always remember. Allison and I reacquainted many years later when we discovered we both live in Alexandria. I'll never forget the day we bumped into each other in the produce aisle at Safeway. I'm so proud of Allison for getting elected and becoming mayor and vice mayor of Alexandria from 2013-2018.

Being elected to the school board of Alexandria City Public Schools in 2006 was an honor of a lifetime. I'm forever grateful for the opportunity to serve the children of the city where I've lived in for the past 27 years and for working alongside my fellow distinguished colleagues, including Sheryl Gorsuch, Ronnie Campbell, Charles Wilson, Mark Williams, Yvonne Folkerts, Arthur Peabody, Blanche Maness, Rebecca Perry, Mort Sherman, John Porter, Mimi Carter, and many others.

My group of dear friends from Brighton High School, whom I'm fortunate to see from time to time in the D.C. area, have been a source of inspiration. I'm grateful for my friendships with Mindy (Friedman) Harrison, Sue (Clark) Martin, Marla (Zucker) McLean, Debbie (Hartman) Galliger, Lisa (Helpert) Tucker, Phyllis (Kurlander) Costanza, Karen Nozik, and Liz (Fine) Porter.

A special thanks to Megan Brown, Sara Vandergoot, and the fabulous instructors and community at Mind the Mat, my yoga and Pilates sanctuary in Del Ray, where I've nourished my body, mind, and soul over the years.

Another big shout-out to Dr. Sean Woods, who helps me stay healthy, and Dalila Benkhouja, who helps me look my best.

I'm deeply grateful to JD Kathuria, founder and CEO of WashingtonExec, for his friendship and support all these years. I can't thank him enough for providing the foreword and for recommending Camille Tuutti to edit this book. Thank you, Camille!

This book wouldn't have happened without the encouragement and mentoring of my good friend, Mark Amtower. We first became acquainted in 2011 when he interviewed me on Federal News Radio. Mark reached out to me about a year ago and urged me to tell my story. His monthly check-ins prodded me along this writing journey. I'm indebted to Mark for his friendship, wise counsel, and great advice.

A huge thanks from the bottom of my heart to Scott Bartley of Bartley & Dick Advertising/Design, an amazing human and designer who created the best book cover I could have ever imagined. Other big thanks to Roslyn Honsberger, a gifted photographer, who captured my "hard talk" personality in some fabulous photos.

I am grateful to Ana Yousuf-Starns, Ph.D. of Cary Press International, whom I was fortunate to meet and who made this book possible. From the moment we talked, I felt we shared a kindred spirit. Thank you, Ana, for holding my hand and making my dream happen.

And last but certainly not least, I'm eternally grateful for my friendship with Stephanie "Steph" Meyer. She's my Aussie soul sister. Back in 2009, when our girls took swimming lessons at the Chinquapin Recreation Center in Alexandria, Andy and I met Steph and her family. She's been an amazing friend over these past 14-plus years. It's been a blast to become a yogi and

Pilatist together. I'm especially thankful to Steph for allowing me to spend many weekends at her beautiful home in Virginia Beach, Virginia, where I've written most of this book. There's something about being at the beach, right? Life *is* better at the beach.

www.ingramcontent.com/pod-product-compliance
Lightning Source LLC
Chambersburg PA
CBHW071211020426

42333CB00015B/1376